MW00932189

STATISTICS
for
College Students
and Researchers

Michael M Nikoletseas, Ph.D.

Second Edition

Copyright © 2020, Michael M. Nikoletseas
ISBN: 979-8588983235

Published in USA

All Rights Reserved. No part of this book may be
reproduced, stored in a retrieval system, or transmitted in
any form, or by any means, electronic, mechanical,
photocopying, recording or otherwise, without prior
permission of the author.

Revision March 2024

PREFACE

The mathematics you will need is very simple arithmetic: addition, subtraction, multiplication and division.

The formulas we will use are very simple and in some instances they do not use symbols, they use words

The number of formulas we will use is five. In fact there is only one formula that you need.

You are wondering whether this book is for college students and researchers or for high school.

The fact is that very few college textbooks cover so many statistical tests, and even fewer present complex statistical designs such as mixed, split-plot designs which are monstrous indeed. Most importantly, very few textbooks teach statistical design.

This book is unique in one more respect.

STATISTICS FOR COLLEGE STUDENTS AND RESEARCHERS

Most people use statistics in real-life environments and not in formal, mathematical domains. Teaching students how to plug in numbers to complex equations, as many textbooks do, is of little help to the graduate student and researcher. As in all fields, you need experience in a real-life research environment.

This book has extended sections that provide this environment.

STATISTICS FOR COLLEGE STUDENTS AND RESEARCHERS

STATISTICS FOR COLLEGE STUDENTS AND RESEARCHERS

V

STATISTICS FOR COLLEGE STUDENTS AND RESEARCHERS

STATISTICS FOR COLLEGE STUDENTS AND RESEARCHERS

VII

STATISTICS FOR COLLEGE STUDENTS
AND RESEARCHERS

PART 1 THEORY CONCEPTS STATISTICAL TESTS

VIII

Statistical tests and other techniques are based on Mathematics. In this part of the book we present the mathematics and the statistical tests that are used in data analysis in the social and natural sciences.

My life long experience in teaching and research has taught me that Statistics cannot be learned in one semester reading a neatly organized textbook and an instructor who has never done research in the natural or social sciences.

I have written this book so that it provided a total environment for the student and researcher in which to do research and grow as intellectuals:

Step by step calculation down to minute detail, development of concepts through real life cases, examples, many examples, lectures in which students interrupt and ask questions, statistical design, practice section, and an addendum for the presentation of a variety of help tips.

What is Statistics

Definition

Statistics is a branch of Mathematics that deals with data. It may be pure Mathematics, probability, or applied Mathematics in which case it is used to organize data (Descriptive Statistics) or make predictions as to the occurrence of an event (Inferential Statistics).

Descriptive Statistics

Descriptive Statistics employs methods and simple arithmetic that allows us to organize our data, for example making graphs or calculating an average.

Inferential Statistics

Inferential Statistics uses methods and more complex mathematical calculations that allow us to make inferences, predictions. Examples of inferential statistics are statistical tests like the t-test.

STATISTICS FOR COLLEGE STUDENTS AND RESEARCHERS

In several fields, including experimental science, prediction takes the form of a probability statement regarding the occurrence of a chance event , the chance event being the finding of an experiment. If the probability that the finding or result of research is a chance event, and not the result of the experimental manipulation is small, then we conclude that the finding of our research is reliable, i.e. it is significant.

Statistics may be further categorized into Parametric and Non-parametric statistics.

Non-parametric Statistics

We choose non-parametric tests when our data are at the nominal or ordinal scale of measurement.

Parametric Statistics

Parametric tests are chosen to analyze data in those instances in which we know that the characteristic we are measuring is normally distributed in the population (for example nose length) and our measurement is ratio or interval scale.Read the print book. Examples of parametric tests are the t-test and analysis of variance.

PARAMETRIC STATISTICS

The averages

There are three "averages" in statistics: the median, the mode, and the mean. Of the three only the mean involves significant calculations and is part of the calculations in all parametric tests of significance.

The median

The median is the middle score in a group of scores that have been ranked in order of magnitude.

The median is that score of the which divides the line of scores into two halves.

Example:
Scores 2 9 4 7 5
Scores ranked 2 4 5 7 9

The score in the middle of the line is 5.
Score 5 is the median.

The mode

The mode is the most frequent value in a range of scores.

Example:
Scores 8 3 5 4 3 9 2 8 3 5 3
Scores ranked 2 3 3 3 3 4 5 5 8 8 9
The most frequent score is 3.
The mode is 3.

The mean

The mean - definition

What is the Mean? The mean (arithmetic mean) or average gives an average of a series of numbers. For example, the average body weight of my friends. All statistical tests require the calculation of the mean as a first step.

The mean - formula

The formula for calculating the mean is

$$\bar{X} = \frac{\sum X}{n}$$

X with the line on top we read: X bar (eks bar). It stands for the mean, the average of the scores in our sample. X stands for score. The capital Greek letter we read: Sigma. It stands for the Sum of the scores. The n we read: n. It stands for the number of scores in our sample.

The mean - example

An experimenter wanted to know what quantity of food young rats eat. weighed the food each ate in 24 hours in grams. He chose 6 rats randomly from the colony of rats in his lab. Here is the data, The symbol for each score is X.

X
34
35
39
30
39
40

Looking at the formula above, we add all of the scores and divide by the number of scores. The symbol for the number of scores is n. In this case the n is 6. The sum of the scores is 217

ΣX=34+35+39*30+39+40=217
Now we divide this by 6, the n, and we find
the mean

$$\bar{X} = \frac{217}{6} = 36.17$$

Variance

What is variance

The definition of variance: Variance is a measure of variability of the scores of our sample, how much they differ from the mean. The concept of variance is most important as it is the basis of statistical tests of significance such as the t-test and analysis of variance, ANOVA.

The formula for variance

The formula for variance is:

$$s^2 = \frac{\sum (X - \bar{X})^2}{n - 1}$$

We read this: variance is the sum of each score from the mean squared, over the sample size minus 1 (n-1). Another way of saying this is: To find variance we subtract each score from the mean and then square this difference. Then we add all of these

STATISTICS FOR COLLEGE STUDENTS AND RESEARCHERS

squared differences and divide by the number of scores minus 1.

The mean - formula

What is the Mean? The mean or average gives an average of a series of numbers. For example, the average body weight of my friends. The formula for calculating the mean is

$$\bar{X} = \frac{\sum X}{n}$$

X with the line on top we read: X bar (eks bar). It stands for the mean, the average of the scores in our sample. X stands for score. The capital Greek letter we read: Sigma. It stands for the Sum of the scores. The n we read: n. It stands for the number of scores in our sample.

Variance -practice example

An experimenter wanted to know what is the variance in the quantity of food young rats eat. He chose 6 rats randomly from the colony of rats in his lab. He weighed the food each ate in 24 hours in grams. Here is the data, The symbol for each score is X.

X 34 35 39 30 39 40

Looking at the variance formula above, we begin by finding the mean, the average. We add all of the scores and divide by the number of scores. The symbol for the number of scores is n. In this case the n is 6. The sum of the scores is 217 . Now we divide this by 6, the n, and we find the mean 36.17.

To compute the variance we have to subtract each score from the mean

$$X - \bar{X}$$

and then square this

$$(X - \bar{X})^2$$

We then sum these squared deviations

$$\sum (X - \bar{X})^2$$

Important! This is the sum of squared deviations of each sore from the mean. It is the SS term on the ANOVA summary table!

Next we divide by n, the number of scores,

$$\frac{\sum (X - \bar{X})^2}{n - 1}$$

This is variance

$$s^2 = \frac{\sum (X - \bar{X})^2}{n - 1}$$

Here are the calculations:

$$X - \bar{X}$$

-2.17 -1.17 2.83 -6.17 2.83 3.83

$$(X - \bar{X})^2$$

$$\sum (X - \bar{X})^2 = 74.8334$$

SUMMARY OF THE ABOVE
CALCULATIONS

X	$X - \bar{X}$	$(X - \bar{X})^2$
34	-2.17	4.7089
35	-1.17	1.3689
39	2.83	8.0089
30	-6.17	38.0689
39	2.83	8.0089
40	3.83	14.6689
ΣX=217 $\bar{X}$=36.1 7		$\sum (X - \bar{X})^2$ =74.8 334

Now we plug in the calculated values above
to the variance formula.

$$s^2 = \frac{\sum (X - \bar{X})^2}{n - 1}$$

$$s^2 = \frac{74.8334}{6 - 1} = 12.47$$

This is the variance of our data.

Standard deviation
Standard deviation definition

Like Variance, it is a measure of
variability of the scores of our sample,
how much they differ from the mean. It is
variance standardized by taking the
square root of variance. We may develop
the concept of standard deviation by
examining the standard normal curve:

The standard normal curve

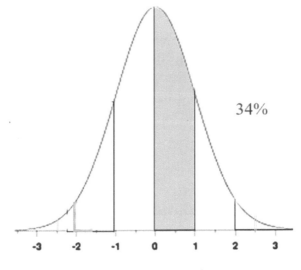

Standard deviation

Observe that in the standard normal curve
there are 3 standard deviations σ on each
side of the mean μ which is 0, The
percentages shown are percentages of the
area under the curve. The total area is 100%.
Knowing the percentage of area between the
mean and a point on the standard deviation
line allows us to calculate the number of
scores contained between these points. In
the graph above, the surface area

between the mean (which is 0) and standard deviation 1 (the gray area) is 34% of the total area. This is the case in the ideal world of the standard normal curve which is generated by a formula. In the real world, in a case in which the curve is generated by plotting data from an experiment, 34% of the scores are between the mean and standard deviation 1.

Standard deviation formula
The formula for standard deviation is:

For population

$$\sigma = \sqrt{\frac{\sum (X - \mu)^2}{N}}$$

μ is the symbol for the population mean.

STATISTICS FOR COLLEGE STUDENTS AND RESEARCHERS

For sample

$$s = \sqrt{\frac{\sum (X - \bar{X})^2}{n - 1}}$$

We read this: Standard deviation is the square root of variance. The symbol for variance is s^2. Variance is the sum of each score from the mean squared, over the sample size minus 1 (n-1). Another way of saying this is: To find variance we subtract each score from the mean and then square this difference. Then we add all of these squared differences and divide by the number of scores minus 1. (Please review the chapter on variance.)

STATISTICS FOR COLLEGE STUDENTS
AND RESEARCHERS

Standard deviation practice example
SUMMARY OF THE ABOVE
CALCULATIONS

X	$X - \bar{X}$	$(X - \bar{X})^2$
34	-2.17	4.7089
35	-1.17	1.3689
39	2.83	8.0089
30	-6.17	38.0689
39	2.83	8.0089
40	3.83	14.6689
$\Sigma X = 217$ $\bar{X}=36.17$		$\sum (X - \bar{X})^2$ =74.8 334

Now we plug in the calculated values above
to the variance formula.

$$s^2 = \frac{\sum (X - \bar{X})^2}{n - 1}$$

$$s^2 = \frac{74.8334}{6 - 1} = 12.47$$

This is the variance of our data.

Finally The formula for standard deviation is:

$$s = \sqrt{\frac{\sum (X - \bar{X})^2}{n - 1}}$$

$$s = \sqrt{s^2}$$

$$s = \sqrt{s^2} = \sqrt{12.47} = 3.53$$

This is the standard deviation of our data.

The standard normal curve

The standard normal curve

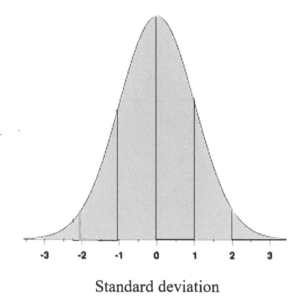

Standard deviation

What is the standard normal curve?

The standard normal curve is a curve that can be generated by an equation. It is bell-shaped, symmetrical, its mean is 0, and it has three standard deviations. The equation that creates the standard normal curve is:

— 23 —

STATISTICS FOR COLLEGE STUDENTS AND RESEARCHERS

$$y = \frac{1}{\sigma\sqrt{2\pi}}e^{\frac{-(\chi-\mu)^2}{2\sigma^2}}$$

The standard normal curve

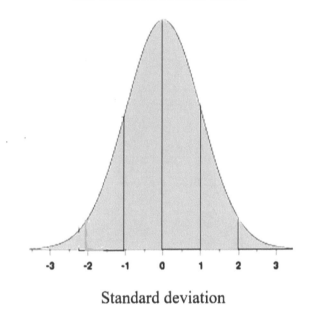

Standard deviation

In the graph above, the gray area covers the entire surface of the curve, 100%.

The following graph shows the percentage of the surface area between the mean and standard deviation 1, which is 34%.

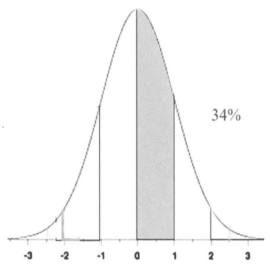

The standard normal curve

34%

Standard deviation

The following graph shows that between standard deviation -2 and +2 ninety-five percent (95%) of the surface area lies.

STATISTICS FOR COLLEGE STUDENTS AND RESEARCHERS

In the graph below, between standard deviation -2.6 and +2.56 ninety-nine percent (99%) of the surface area lies,

The standard normal curve

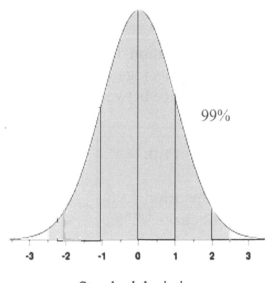

Standard deviation

How is the standard normal curve used

- Normal distribution, use number 1. To describe, to organize data

STATISTICS FOR COLLEGE STUDENTS AND RESEARCHERS

- Normal distribution, use number 2. Making statements of probability, betting

- Normal distribution, use number 3. To make statements regarding the reliability of a single mean

- Normal distribution, use number 4. To make statements regarding the reliability of the difference between two means.

Important tip:

Standard deviation 1.96
Percent of curve 95%

Standard deviation 2.56
Percent of curve 99%

Always remember this.

/
The normal-distribution table - how to use

The Normal Curve Table

Z	0.00	0.01	0.02	0.03	0.04	0.05	0.06	0.07	0.08	0.09
0.0	0.0000	0.0040	0.0080	0.0120	0.0160	0.0199	0.0239	0.0279	0.0319	0.0359
0.1	0.0398	0.0438	0.0478	0.0517	0.0557	0.0596	0.0636	0.0675	0.0714	0.0753
0.2	0.0793	0.0832	0.0871	0.0910	0.0948	0.0987	0.1026	0.1064	0.1103	0.1141
0.3	0.1179	0.1217	0.1255	0.1293	0.1331	0.1368	0.1406	0.1443	0.1480	0.1517
0.4	0.1554	0.1591	0.1628	0.1664	0.1700	0.1736	0.1772	0.1808	0.1844	0.1879
0.5	0.1915	0.1950	0.1985	0.2019	0.2054	0.2088	0.2123	0.2157	0.2190	0.2224
0.6	0.2257	0.2291	0.2324	0.2357	0.2389	0.2422	0.2454	0.2486	0.2517	0.2549
0.7	0.2580	0.2611	0.2642	0.2673	0.2704	0.2734	0.2764	0.2794	0.2823	0.2852
0.8	0.2881	0.2910	0.2939	0.2967	0.2995	0.3023	0.3051	0.3078	0.3106	0.3133
0.9	0.3159	0.3186	0.3212	0.3238	0.3264	0.3289	0.3315	0.3340	0.3365	0.3389
1.0	0.3413	0.3438	0.3461	0.3485	0.3508	0.3531	0.3554	0.3577	0.3599	0.3621
1.1	0.3643	0.3665	0.3686	0.3708	0.3729	0.3749	0.3770	0.3790	0.3810	0.3830
1.2	0.3849	0.3869	0.3888	0.3907	0.3925	0.3944	0.3962	0.3980	0.3997	0.4015
1.3	0.4032	0.4049	0.4066	0.4082	0.4099	0.4115	0.4131	0.4147	0.4162	0.4177
1.4	0.4192	0.4207	0.4222	0.4236	0.4251	0.4265	0.4279	0.4292	0.4306	0.4319
1.5	0.4332	0.4345	0.4357	0.4370	0.4382	0.4394	0.4406	0.4418	0.4429	0.4441
1.6	0.4452	0.4463	0.4474	0.4484	0.4495	0.4505	0.4515	0.4525	0.4535	0.4545
1.7	0.4554	0.4564	0.4573	0.4582	0.4591	0.4599	0.4608	0.4616	0.4625	0.4633
1.8	0.4641	0.4649	0.4656	0.4664	0.4671	0.4678	0.4686	0.4693	0.4699	0.4706
1.9	0.4713	0.4719	0.4726	0.4732	0.4738	0.4744	0.4750	0.4756	0.4761	0.4767
2.0	0.4772	0.4778	0.4783	0.4788	0.4793	0.4798	0.4803	0.4808	0.4812	0.4817
2.1	0.4821	0.4826	0.4830	0.4834	0.4838	0.4842	0.4846	0.4850	0.4854	0.4857
2.2	0.4861	0.4864	0.4868	0.4871	0.4875	0.4878	0.4881	0.4884	0.4887	0.4890
2.3	0.4893	0.4896	0.4898	0.4901	0.4904	0.4906	0.4909	0.4911	0.4913	0.4916
2.4	0.4918	0.4920	0.4922	0.4925	0.4927	0.4929	0.4931	0.4932	0.4934	0.4936
2.5	0.4938	0.4940	0.4941	0.4943	0.4945	0.4946	0.4948	0.4949	0.4951	0.4952
2.6	0.4953	0.4955	0.4956	0.4957	0.4959	0.4960	0.4961	0.4962	0.4963	0.4964
2.7	0.4965	0.4966	0.4967	0.4968	0.4969	0.4970	0.4971	0.4972	0.4973	0.4974
2.8	0.4974	0.4975	0.4976	0.4977	0.4977	0.4978	0.4979	0.4979	0.4980	0.4981
9	0.4981	0.4982	0.4982	0.4983	0.4984	0.4984	0.4985	0.4985	0.4986	0.4986
3.0	0.4987	0.4987	0.4987	0.4988	0.4988	0.4989	0.4989	0.4989	0.4990	0.4990

STATISTICS FOR COLLEGE STUDENTS AND RESEARCHERS

Example: Place your finger at 1.9 on the first left column. Draw your finger horizontally to the seventh column. You read 0.4750 . This means that between the mean and standard deviation or z 1.96 47.5% of the area of the curve lies.

Standard error of the mean

The standard error of the mean (SEM) is an estimate of the standard deviation of a curve that would be graphing means of samples repeatedly taken. It is used routinely in graphs and tables of means of actual experimental data. .

For example, $Mean = 23.5 \pm 1.25$

Here the standard error of the mean is 1.25

The problem

A coach wanted to know the mean (average) height of male freshmen. He also wants to know how much these heights vary, and how reliable the mean is, that is will he get approximately the same mean if he measures again? He took a sample and measured their heights in cm.

X
1.88
1.86
2.00
11.9
1.78
1.85
1.87
1.98
1.82
1.90
1.76

The formula for SEM is simple:

$$SEM = \frac{\sigma}{\sqrt{n}}$$

He will calculate the mean and standard deviation (see chapters on variance and standard deviation) and then divide the standard deviation by the square root of the number of scores.

STATISTICS FOR COLLEGE STUDENTS AND RESEARCHERS

N=11
Mean: 2.78
$s2 = 9.15$

$a = \sqrt{s2} = \sqrt{9.15} = 3.03$

$SEM = s/\sqrt{N} = 3.03/\sqrt{11} = 0.91$

He will report the mean as follows

$$Mean = 2.78 \pm 0.91$$

The t-test

The t-test is used to analyze data from experiments which have two groups. It is used in order to decide whether the difference between group 1 and group 2 is real or a chance event. Another way of saying this is: the t-test is used in order to decide whether the difference between mean of group 1 and mean of group 2 is reliable. In statistical jargon we say that we test to see whether the difference is significant.

t-test -formula

The formula for t-test is:

$$t = \frac{\bar{X}_1 - \bar{X}_2}{\sqrt{\frac{s_1{}^2}{n_1}} + \sqrt{\frac{s_2{}^2}{n_2}}}$$

To calculate the t, we need to first calculate the mean and the variance. The formula for the mean is:

$$\bar{X} = \frac{\sum X}{n}$$

The formula for variance is

$$s^2 = \frac{\sum (X - \bar{X})^2}{n - 1}$$

Examples for the calculations were given in the chapters on the mean and variance.

t-test practice example

A psychologist wanted to test the effects of two vitamins on hand steadiness of male teenagers. He randomly selected 12 subjects and randomly assigned them to two groups, 6 each. Group 1 received vitamin 1 for two weeks and then each subject was asked to shoot an arrow to a target. The distance from the center of the target that the arrow hit was recorded in cm The same method was followed with Group 2, each subject of which received vitamin 2. lower scores indicate better hand steadiness. The data were analyzed by using a t-test for independent groups.

STATISTICS FOR COLLEGE STUDENTS AND RESEARCHERS

Group 1	Group 2
34	48
35	47
39	45
30	47
39	46
940	45
Mean= 36.17	Mean= 46.33
Variance s_1^2= 12.47	Variance s_2^2= 1.22
n1= 6	n2= 6

Now we plug in the values of our calculation into the t formula.

$$t = \frac{36.17 - 46.33}{\sqrt{\frac{12.47}{6}} + \sqrt{\frac{1.22}{6}}}$$

t=7.31

df= 6+6-2=10
p<0.05

STATISTICS FOR COLLEGE STUDENTS AND RESEARCHERS

The final step is to go to the t table and enter at the 0.05 level with degrees of freedom 10.

The value we find is 1.81, which is less than the value of the t we calculated t=7.31. We express this as p<0.05. We conclude that the difference between the two means is significant. This means that our finding is reliable and not a chance event.

STATISTICS FOR COLLEGE STUDENTS AND RESEARCHERS

The t-distribution table

One-sided	75%	80%	85%	90%	95%	97.50%	99%	99.50%	99.75%	99.90%	99.95%
Two-sided	50%	60%	70%	80%	90%	95%	98%	99%	99.50%	99.80%	99.90%
1	1	1.376	1.963	3.078	6.314	12.71	31.82	63.66	127.3	318.3	636.6
2	0.816	1.08	1.386	1.886	2.92	4.303	6.965	9.925	14.09	22.33	31.6
3	0.765	0.978	1.25	1.638	2.353	3.182	4.541	5.841	7.453	10.21	12.92
4	0.741	0.941	1.19	1.533	2.132	2.776	3.747	4.604	5.598	7.173	8.61
5	0.727	0.92	1.156	1.476	2.015	2.571	3.365	4.032	4.773	5.893	6.869
6	0.718	0.906	1.134	1.44	1.943	2.447	3.143	3.707	4.317	5.208	5.959
7	0.711	0.896	1.119	1.415	1.895	2.365	2.998	3.499	4.029	4.785	5.408
8	0.706	0.889	1.108	1.397	1.86	2.306	2.896	3.355	3.833	4.501	5.041
9	0.703	0.883	1.1	1.383	1.833	2.262	2.821	3.25	3.69	4.297	4.781
10	0.7	0.879	1.093	1.372	1.812	2.228	2.764	3.169	3.581	4.144	4.587
11	0.697	0.876	1.088	1.363	1.796	2.201	2.718	3.106	3.497	4.025	4.437
12	0.695	0.873	1.083	1.356	1.782	2.179	2.681	3.055	3.428	3.93	4.318
13	0.694	0.87	1.079	1.35	1.771	2.16	2.65	3.012	3.372	3.852	4.221
14	0.692	0.868	1.076	1.345	1.761	2.145	2.624	2.977	3.326	3.787	4.14
15	0.691	0.866	1.074	1.341	1.753	2.131	2.602	2.947	3.286	3.733	4.073
16	0.69	0.865	1.071	1.337	1.746	2.12	2.583	2.921	3.252	3.686	4.015
17	0.689	0.863	1.069	1.333	1.74	2.11	2.567	2.898	3.222	3.646	3.965
18	0.688	0.862	1.067	1.33	1.734	2.101	2.552	2.878	3.197	3.61	3.922
19	0.688	0.861	1.066	1.328	1.729	2.093	2.539	2.861	3.174	3.579	3.883
20	0.687	0.86	1.064	1.325	1.725	2.086	2.528	2.845	3.153	3.552	3.85
21	0.686	0.859	1.063	1.323	1.721	2.08	2.518	2.831	3.135	3.527	3.819
22	0.686	0.858	1.061	1.321	1.717	2.074	2.508	2.819	3.119	3.505	3.792
23	0.685	0.858	1.06	1.319	1.714	2.069	2.5	2.807	3.104	3.485	3.767
24	0.685	0.857	1.059	1.318	1.711	2.064	2.492	2.797	3.091	3.467	3.745
25	0.684	0.856	1.058	1.316	1.708	2.06	2.485	2.787	3.078	3.45	3.725
26	0.684	0.856	1.058	1.315	1.706	2.056	2.479	2.779	3.067	3.435	3.707
27	0.684	0.855	1.057	1.314	1.703	2.052	2.473	2.771	3.057	3.421	3.69
28	0.683	0.855	1.056	1.313	1.701	2.048	2.467	2.763	3.047	3.408	3.674
29	0.683	0.854	1.055	1.311	1.699	2.045	2.462	2.756	3.038	3.396	3.659
30	0.683	0.854	1.055	1.31	1.697	2.042	2.457	2.75	3.03	3.385	3.646
40	0.681	0.851	1.05	1.303	1.684	2.021	2.423	2.704	2.971	3.307	3.551
50	0.679	0.849	1.047	1.299	1.676	2.009	2.403	2.678	2.937	3.261	3.496
60	0.679	0.848	1.045	1.296	1.671	2	2.39	2.66	2.915	3.232	3.46
80	0.678	0.846	1.043	1.292	1.664	1.99	2.374	2.639	2.887	3.195	3.416
100	0.677	0.845	1.042	1.29	1.66	1.984	2.364	2.626	2.871	3.174	3.39
120	0.677	0.845	1.041	1.289	1.658	1.98	2.358	2.617	2.86	3.16	3.373
∞	0.674	0.842	1.036	1.282	1.645	1.96	2.326	2.576	2.807	3.09	3.291

One-sided	75%	80%	85%	90%	95%	97.50%	99%	99.50%	99.75%	99.90%	99.95%
Two-sided	50%	60%	70%	80%	90%	95%	98%	99%	99.50%	99.80%	99.90%

STATISTICS FOR COLLEGE STUDENTS AND RESEARCHERS

How to use the t-table, an example.

An experiment has 2 groups of subjects, 6 subjects in each group, 12 subjects total. Group 1 received a placebo (an inert substance). Group 2 received a drug. The temperature of each subject was recorded. We have 12 scores, 6 scores in each group.

Step 1. We calculate the means, mean 1 and mean 2.
Step 2. We calculate the degrees of freedom, df, it is 10. How do we calculate df?

df=total number of scores minus the number of means. In this case 12-2=10.
Step 3. We run the t-test for independent groups and, suppose, we find that t=4.52. We call this the calculated t.
Step 4. Now we go to the t-table and enter the left column at df 10.

We now slide our finger to the right as far as the column with the heading 95% two sided (also called two tailed). The number we see here is 2.228. We call this the required t.
Step 5. We now compare our calculated t to

the required t, i.e.the t in the table.
Calculated t=4.53. Required t=2.22.
The calculated t is greater than the required
t, i.e. the table t.

We conclude that we have significance. This
means that the difference between mean 1
and mean 2 is significant (loosely speaking
that it is real and not a chance event). We
report this as follows:
$p < 0.05$ P less than point o five.

Paired t-test

The paired t-test is used to analyze data from experiments in which there is only one group of subjects and each subject was given two treatments.It is c;ear that each subject gives two scores, which are correlated, they are not independent (they do not come from different subjects..

Paired t-test formula

The formula for the paired samples t-test is:

$$t_{paired} = \frac{\bar{X}_D}{\sqrt{\frac{s^2}{n}}}$$

We read this: t paired equals mean of the differences minus mean over standard deviation divided by the square root of sample size n.

STATISTICS FOR COLLEGE STUDENTS
AND RESEARCHERS

Paired t-test-practice example

An experimenter wanted to find the effect of a new drug, Y13, on hand steadiness. He randomly selected seven subjects and tested their accuracy of hitting a target. He measured how many centimeters the shot deviated from the center of the target. He then gave each subject the drug, waited for one hour and repeated the shooting test. He recorded again the distance that the shot deviated from the center of the target. He now had two scores for each subject, one before the drug, and one after the drug. Here are the scores in a table,

STATISTICS FOR COLLEGE STUDENTS AND RESEARCHERS

Subjects	Pre Drug	Post Drug	D (Post--Pre)	D-Mean	(D-Mean) squared
1	4	5	1	-0.86	\0.73
2	2	3	1	-0.86	0.73
3	6	8	2	0.14	0.02
4	4	5	1	-0.86	0.73
5	2	5	3	1.31	
6	3	6	3	1.14	1.31
7	6	8	2	1.14	0.02
				0.14	

	Mean= 1.86	SUM= 4.86

The formula for t paired test is

$$t_{paired} = \frac{\bar{X}_D}{\sqrt{\frac{s^2}{n}}}$$

Next we plug in the formula the calculations from the above table

$$t_{paired} = \frac{1.86}{0.33}$$

t=1.86/0.33=5.6

The last step is to go to t- table and enter with degrees of freedom df=12 at the 0.05 level of significance. The t value in the t table is 1.8. We compare this with the t value of our calculations, which is 5.6. Because this is greater than the t of the table (5.6>1.8 (we conclude that we have significance. The two means are significantly different. The drug had an effect on hand stability. In our report of our experiment we include the p value as follows: p<0.05. We read this: p less than 0.05.

Note: The paired t-test is also called t-test for dependent means, paired samples t-test, matched pairs t-test.

STATISTICS FOR COLLEGE STUDENTS
AND RESEARCHERS

Analysis of Variance ANOVA

Analysis of Variance, ANOVA, is used to
analyze data from experiments which have
two or more groups. It is used in order to
decide whether the difference between
group 1 and group 2 is real or a chance
event. Another way of saying this is: the
ANOVA is used in order to decide whether
the difference between mean of group 1 and
mean of group 2 is reliable. In statistical
jargon we say that we test to see whether the
difference is significant.

Analysis of Variance ANOVA -formula

The formula for ANOVA is:

$$F = \frac{MS_{between}}{MS_{within}}$$

We read this as follows: Mean square
between over mean square within. What is
mean square, you ask? It is the mean of
squares. What is squares, you ask. Squares is
the statistical term for squared deviations (of
squared differences) of each score X from
the mean. What are the squared differences,
you ask. Remember the formula for
variance?

$$s^2 = \frac{\sum (X - \bar{X})^2}{n}$$

Look at the numerator
$\sum (X - \bar{X})^2$ These are the squared
differences or summed. To complete our
reasoning, we go back to where we started,
the F formula, or F ratio, the formula for
ANOVA. Why mean sums of squares?
Simple because like all averages, we divide
by the number of scores. If you are
observant, you will notice that the F formula
is a modified t formula.

STATISTICS FOR COLLEGE STUDENTS AND RESEARCHERS

Analysis of variance (ANOVA) practice example

Group 1	Group 2	Group 3
200	204	214
203	210	220
199	214	225
190	219	220
204	211	229
---------	---------	---------
n1: 5	n2: 5	n3: 5
df1 = n-1= 5-1= 4	df2 = n - 1 = 5 - 1 = 4	df3 = n - 1 = 5 - 1 = 4
Mean1: 199.2	Mean2: 211.6	Mean3: 221.6
SS1: 122.8	SS2: 121.2	SS3: 129.2
s_1^2 = SS1/(n - 1) = 122.8/(5-1) = 30.7	s_2^2 = SS2/(n - 1) = 121.2/(5-1) = 30.3	s_3^2 = SS3/(b - 1) = 129.2/(5-1) = 32.3

What is df? df stands for degrees of freedom. The simplest way to grasp this concept is to think of a game in which a list of numbers is hidden except for the n (how many) and the mean. You are asked to draw one number and asked to guess the number. Of course, you cannot guess it. When you draw the last number, you are asked to guess it, and of course you can guess it. At this point, there are no more degrees of freedom What you should remember is:

Every time you calculate a mean, you lose 1 degree of freedom. df= n-1

ANOVA SUMMARY TABLE

Source	SS	df	MS	F	p
Between	1259	2	629.6	20.24	<0.0001
Within	373.2	12	31.10		
Total	1632	14			

After we calculate the F, we go to the F tables and enter with the degrees of freedom we have, in this case 2 and 12. We first check the 0.05 level (level of significance). If our F is greater than the one in the F table, we say $p<0.05$, p less than 0.05. It has been accepted among scientists that at the 0.05

level we are allowed to say that we have
significance, that the finding of our
experiment is reliable.

The F-distribution table - how to use

The F distribution Table 5% significance level

	1	2	3	4	5	6	7	8	9	10
1	161.4	199.5	215.7	224.5	230.1	233.9	236.7	238.8	240.5	241.8
2	18.51	19.00	19.16	19.24	19.29	19.33	19.35	19.37	19.38	19.39
3	10.12	9.552	9.277	9.117	9.013	8.941	8.887	8.845	8.812	8.786
4	7.709	6.944	6.591	6.388	6.256	6.163	6.094	6.041	5.999	5.964
5	6.608	5.786	5.409	5.192	5.050	4.950	4.876	4.818	4.772	4.735
6	5.987	5.143	4.757	4.534	4.387	4.284	4.207	4.147	4.099	4.060
7	5.591	4.737	4.347	4.120	3.972	3.866	3.787	3.726	3.677	3.637
8	5.318	4.459	4.066	3.838	3.687	3.581	3.500	3.438	3.388	3.347
9	5.117	4.256	3.863	3.633	3.482	3.374	3.293	3.230	3.179	3.137
10	4.965	4.103	3.708	3.478	3.326	3.217	3.135	3.072	3.020	2.978
11	4.844	3.982	3.587	3.357	3.204	3.095	3.012	2.948	2.896	2.854
12	4.747	3.885	3.490	3.259	3.106	2.996	2.913	2.849	2.796	2.753F
13	4.667	3.806	3.411	3.179	3.025	2.915	2.832	2.767	2.714	2.671
14	4.600	3.739	3.344	3.112	2.958	2.848	2.764	2.699	2.646	2.602
15	4.543	3.682	3.287	3.056	2.901	2.790	2.707	2.641	2.588	2.544
16	4.494	3.634	3.239	3.007	2.852	2.741	2.657	2.591	2.538	2.494
17	4.451	3.592	3.197	2.965	2.810	2.699	2.614	2.548	2.494	2.450
18	4.414	3.555	3.160	2.928	2.773	2.661	2.577	2.510	2.456	2.412
19	4.381	3.522	3.127	2.895	2.740	2.628	2.544	2.477	2.423	2.378
20	4.351	3.493	3.098	2.866	2.711	2.599	2.514	2.447	2.393	2.348
21	4.325	3.467	3.072	2.840	2.685	2.573	2.488	2.420	2.366	2.321
22	4.301	3.443	3.049	2.817	2.661	2.549	2.464	2.397	2.342	2.297
23	4.279	3.422	3.028	2.796	2.640	2.528	2.442	2.375	2.320	2.275
24	4.260	3.403	3.009	2.776	2.621	2.508	2.423	2.355	2.300	2.255
25	4.242	3.385	2.991	2.759	2.603	2.490	2.405	2.337	2.282	2.236
26	4.225	3.369	2.975	2.743	2.587	2.474	2.388	2.321	2.265	2.220
27	4.210	3.354	2.960	2.728	2.572	2.459	2.373	2.305	2.250	2.204

STATISTICS FOR COLLEGE STUDENTS AND RESEARCHERS

28	4.196	3.340	2.947	2.714	2.558	2.445	2.359	2.291	2.236 2.190
29	4.183	3.328	2.934	2.701	2.545	2.432	2.346	2.278	2.223 2.177
30	4.171	3.316	2.922	2.690	2.534	2.421	2.334	2.266	2.211 2.165
31	4.160	3.305	2.911	2.679	2.523	2.409	2.323	2.255	2.199 2.153
32	4.149	3.295	2.901	2.668	2.512	2.399	2.313	2.244	2.189 2.142
33	4.139	3.285	2.892	2.659	2.503	2.389	2.303	2.235	2.179 2.133
34	4.130	3.276	2.883	2.650	2.494	2.380	2.294	2.225	2.170 2.123
35	4.121	3.267	2.874	2.641	2.485	2.372	2.285	2.217	2.161 2.114
36	4.113	3.259	2.866	2.634	2.477	2.364	2.277	2.209	2.153 2.106
37	4.105	3.252	2.859	2.626	2.470	2.356	2.270	2.201	2.145 2.0
38	4.098	3.245	2.852	2.619	2.463	2.349	2.262	2.194	2.138 2.091
39	4.091	3.238	2.845	2.612	2.456	2.342	2.255	2.187	2.131 2.084
40	4.085	3.232	2.839	2.606	2.449	2.336	2.249	2.180	2.124 2.077
41	4.079	3.226	2.833	2.600	2.443	2.330	2.243	2.174	2.118 2.071
42	4.073	3.220	2.827	2.594	2.438	2.324	2.237	2.168	2.112 2.065
43	4.067	3.214	2.822	2.589	2.432	2.318	2.232	2.163	2.106 2.059
44	4.062	3.209	2.816	2.584	2.427	2.313	2.226	2.157	2.101 2.054
45	4.057	3.204	2.812	2.579	2.422	2.308	2.221	2.152	2.096 2.049
46	4.052	3.200	2.807	2.574	2.417	2.304	2.216	2.147	2.091 2.044
47	4.047	3.195	2.802	2.570	2.413	2.299	2.212	2.143	2.086 2.039
48	4.043	3.191	2.798	2.565	2.409	2.295	2.207	2.138	2.082 2.035
49	4.038	3.187	2.794	2.561	2.404	2.290	2.203	2.134	2.077 2.030
50	4.034	3.183	2.790	2.557	2.400	2.286	2.199	2.130	2.073 2.026
51	4.030	3.179	2.786	2.553	2.397	2.283	2.195	2.126	2.069 2.022
52	4.027	3.175	2.783	2.550	2.393	2.279	2.192	2.122	2.066 2.018
53	4.023	3.172	2.779	2.546	2.389	2.275	2.188	2.119	2.062 2.015
54	4.020	3.168	2.776	2.543	2.386	2.272	2.185	2.115	2.059 2.011
55	4.016	3.165	2.773	2.540	2.383	2.269	2.181	2.112	2.055 2.008
56	4.013	3.162	2.769	2.537	2.380	2.266	2.178	2.109	2.052 2.005
57	4.010	3.159	2.766	2.534	2.377	2.263	2.175	2.106	2.049 2.001
58	4.007	3.156	2.764	2.531	2.374	2.260	2.172	2.103	2.046 1.998
59	4.004	3.153	2.761	2.528	2.371	2.257	2.169	2.100	2.043 1.995
60	4.001	3.150	2.758	2.525	2.368	2.254	2.167	2.097	2.040 1.993
61	3.998	3.148	2.755	2.523	2.366	2.251	2.164	2.094	2.037 1.990
62	3.996	3.145	2.753	2.520	2.363	2.249	2.161	2.092	2.035 1.987
63	3.993	3.143	2.751	2.518	2.361	2.246	2.159	2.089	2.032 1.985
64	3.991	3.140	2.748	2.515	2.358	2.244	2.156	2.087	2.030 1.982
65	3.989	3.138	2.746	2.513	2.356	2.242	2.154	2.084	2.027 1.980
66	3.986	3.136	2.744	2.511	2.354	2.239	2.152	2.082	2.025 1.977
67	3.984	3.134	2.742	2.509	2.352	2.237	2.150	2.080	2.023 1.975
68	3.982	3.132	2.740	2.507	2.350	2.235	2.148	2.078	2.021 1.973
69	3.980	3.130	2.737	2.505	2.348	2.233	2.145	2.076	2.019 1.971

STATISTICS FOR COLLEGE STUDENTS AND RESEARCHERS

70	3.978	3.128	2.736	2.503	2.346	2.231	2.143	2.074	2.017 1.969
71	3.976	3.126	2.734	2.501	2.344	2.229	2.142	2.072	2.015 1.967
72	3.974	3.124	2.732	2.499	2.342	2.227	2.140	2.070	2.013 1.965
73	3.972	3.122	2.730	2.497	2.340	2.226	2.138	2.068	2.011 1.963
74	3.970	3.120	2.728	2.495	2.338	2.224	2.136	2.066	2.009 1.961
75	3.968	3.119	2.727	2.494	2.337	2.222	2.134	2.064	2.007 1.959
76	3.967	3.117	2.725	2.492	2.335	2.220	2.133	2.063	2.006 1.958
77	3.965	3.115	2.723	2.490	2.333	2.219	2.131	2.061	2.004 1.956
78	3.963	3.114	2.722	2.489	2.332	2.217	2.129	2.059	2.002 1.954
79	3.962	3.112	2.720	2.487	2.330	2.216	2.128	2.058	2.001 1.953
80	3.960	3.111	2.719	2.486	2.329	2.214	2.126	2.056	1.999 1.951
81	3.959	3.109	2.717	2.484	2.327	2.213	2.125	2.055	1.998 1.950
82	3.957	3.108	2.716	2.483	2.326	2.211	2.123	2.053	1.996 1.948
83	3.956	3.107	2.715	2.482	2.324	2.210	2.122	2.052	1.995 1.947
84	3.955	3.105	2.713	2.480	2.323	2.209	2.121	2.051	1.993 1.945
85	3.953	3.104	2.712	2.479	2.322	2.207	2.119	2.049	1.992 1.944
86	3.952	3.103	2.711	2.478	2.321	2.206	2.118	2.048	1.991 1.943
87	3.951	3.101	2.709	2.476	2.319	2.205	2.117	2.047	1.989 1.941
88	3.949	3.100	2.708	2.475	2.318	2.203	2.115	2.045	1.988 1.940
89	3.948	3.099	2.707	2.474	2.317	2.202	2.114	2.044	1.987 1.939
90	3.947	3.098	2.706	2.473	2.316	2.201	2.113	2.043	1.986 1.938
91	3.946	3.097	2.705	2.472	2.315	2.200	2.112	2.042	1.984 1.936
92	3.945	3.095	2.704	2.471	2.313	2.199	2.111	2.041	1.983 1.935
93	3.943	3.094	2.703	2.470	2.312	2.198	2.110	2.040	1.982 1.934
94	3.942	3.093	2.701	2.469	2.311	2.197	2.109	2.038	1.981 1.933
95	3.941	3.092	2.700	2.467	2.310	2.196	2.108	2.037	1.980 1.932
96	3.940	3.091	2.699	2.466	2.309	2.195	2.106	2.036	1.979 1.931
97	3.939	3.090	2.698	2.465	2.308	2.194	2.105	2.035	1.978 1.930
98	3.938	3.089	2.697	2.465	2.307	2.193	2.104	2.034	1.977 1.929
99	3.937	3.088	2.696	2.464	2.306	2.192	2.103	2.033	1.976 1.928
100	3.936	3.087	2.696	2.463	2.305	2.191	2.103	2.032	1.975 1.927

How to use the F-table
The first, left column is the df (degrees of freedom) of the denominator of the F ratio, (also called the error term.
The first, top line is the degrees of freedom of the numerator of the F ratio.

Example:

In an experiment with 3 groups, of 10 subjects each, we have df between 2, and df within 27.
Suppose that we analyzed our data using ANOVA and we found an F=12.54. We call this the computed F.
Now we enter the F table. Place your finger on the first left column at 27, then draw your finger to the third column which has the heading 2. You read the value 3.354 We call this the required F.

Now you compare your computed F which was F=12.54 to the required F of this table which is 3.354 Your computed F is bigger, so the finding of your experiment is

STATISTICS FOR COLLEGE STUDENTS
AND RESEARCHERS

significant, p<0.05.
In scientific reports, we always report this p value.

2 x 2 factorial Analysis of

Variance ANOVA

In single-factor, one-way ANOVA, two or
more groups of subjects each receive one
treatment consisting of a single factor. In
factorial designs 4 or more groups of
subjects each receive a treatment which
consists of two or more factors combined.

The layout of these designs are given below.

The layout of a single factor ANOVA

Group 1	Group 2
Subject 1	Subject 6
Subject 2	Subject 7
Subject 3	Subject 8
Subject 4	Subject 9
Subject 5	Subject 10

STATISTICS FOR COLLEGE STUDENTS
AND RESEARCHERS

In this example, Group 1 received a sugar
pill, Group 2 received a new drug, Drugx.It
is important to note that the subjects of
group 1 do not receive Drugx. Similarly the
subjects of group 2 do not receive the sugar
pill. This is the concept of independence, an
important concept in Statistics.

The layout of a 2x2 factorial ANOVA

	B1	B2
A1	A1B1 Subject 1 Subject 2 Subject 3 Subject 4 Subject 5	A1B2 Subject 6 Subject 7 Subject 8 Subject 9 Subject 10
A2	A2B1 Subject 11 Subject 12 Subject 13 Subject 14 Subject 15	A2B2 Subject 16 Subject 17 Subject 18 Subject 19 Subject 20

In this example of a factorial design, we
have a 2x2 (we read this as "a two by two")
factorial. A two by two, meaning two factors
A and B with two levels each. In another
case of a 2x3 factorial design we have two
factors, A and B, factor A two levels, factor
B three levels.

STATISTICS FOR COLLEGE STUDENTS AND RESEARCHERS

STATISTICS FOR COLLEGE STUDENTS AND RESEARCHERS

FORMAT OF 2x2 FACTORIAL ANOVA
SUMMARY TABLE

Source	SS	df	MS	F	p
Between A					
Between B					
AxB (interaction)					
Within					
Total					

Interaction -factorial designs

Note the term "Interaction" in the ANOVA summary table of the factorial design What is interaction? The best way to grasp the concept of interaction is to graph it.

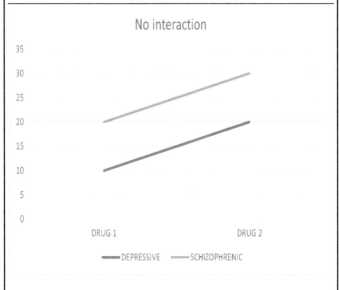

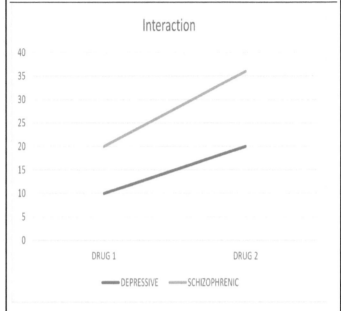

Interaction

ANOVA 2x2 factorial practice example

An experimenter wanted to test the effect of two drugs on the emotionality of male and female teenagers. He randomly selected 10 male and 10 female teenagers and randomly assigned them to 4 groups: Group 1, Group 2, Group 3, Group 4, five subjects in each group as shown in the following table.

STATISTICS FOR COLLEGE STUDENTS AND RESEARCHERS

	Drug 1 B1	Drug 2 B2
Male A1	A1B1 Group1 Subject 1 Subject 2 Subject 3 Subject 4 Subject 5	A1B2 Group2 Subject 6 Subject 7 Subject 8 Subject 9 Subject 10
Female A2	A2B1 Group3 Subject 11 Subject 12 Subject 13 Subject 14 Subject 15	A2B2 Group4 Subject 16 Subject 17 Subject 18 Subject 19 Subject 20

The data are presented on the table below. The scores are the values recorded on a device measuring galvanic skin response, a

STATISTICS FOR COLLEGE STUDENTS AND RESEARCHERS

measure of emotionality. Higher values indicate stronger emotion.

	B1	B2
A1	A1B1	A1B2
	11	17
	11	18
	13	17
	12	16
	10	17
A2	A2B1	A2B2
	15	20
	14	19
	14	18
	16	20
	15	18

.

STATISTICS FOR COLLEGE STUDENTS AND RESEARCHERS

2x2 FACTORIAL ANOVA SUMMARY TABLE

Source	SS	df	MS	F	p
Between A	36.45	1	36.45	41.66	<0.0001
Between B	120.05	1	120.05	137.2	<0.0001
AxB (interaction)	2.45	1	2.45	2.8	>0.95
Within	14	16	0.88		
Total	172.95	19			

After we calculate the F, we go to the F tables and enter with the degrees of freedom we have, in this case 1 and 16. We first check the 0.05 level (level of significance). The F at df 1 and 16 is 4.49. In the summary table we see that the F for factor A is 41.66. This is greater than 4.49, so we conclude that here we have significance at the 0.05

STATISTICS FOR COLLEGE STUDENTS AND RESEARCHERS

level of significance; we say p<0.05, p less than 0.05. It has been accepted among scientists that at the 0.05 level we are allowed to say that we have significance, that the finding of our experiment is reliable.

Next we look at factor B. We see df 1 and 16 and F=137.2. We go to the F table and enter with df 1 and 16 and find F 4.49. This is less than 137.2, therefore we conclude that we have significance at the 0.05 level. We formally express this as follows: p<0.05.

Next we look at AxB. We see df 1 and 16 and F=2.8. This is less than the F table value of 4.49 so we conclude that here we do not have significance. We formally express this as follows: p>0.05.

Step by step calculation of 2x2 ANOVA factorial

The goal of our calculations in ANOVA is to compute the F ratio, The F ratio is MS between over MS within. Mean Square is the mean of the squared deviations (differences) of each score from the mean. These are very simple calculations involving high school mathematics. Simple as they are, they are very important concepts in data analysis and beyond, that is science in general. You will never need to perform these calculations. There are many free Statistics calculators online. However, for the purpose of developing the concepts of ANOVA here are the steps:

1. Calculate the mean of each group.
2. Subtract each score from the mean.
3. Square each difference
4. Add these squared differences.
(This is the Sum of Squares, the SS on the ANOVA summary table.)
5. calculate the degrees of freedom df (number of scores that went into the calculation of the mean minus 1)
6 Divide the SS by the df. Voila! this the MS.
7. The last step is to calculate the F. Divide MS by the MS of the error term (which is the MS within but may be something else depending on which ANOVA design you have.)

The F ratio, as all ratios, compare two things. For example the ratio 8/4 compares 8 to 4 and finds that 8 is two times greater than 4.

Understanding the 2x2 factorial ANOVA summary table

A

Looking at the layout tables above, we see that factor A is gender. Factor B is drug. Our calculations gave a p value <0.05 meaning that factor A, gender, gave a significant difference. In other words, there is a difference in emotionality between male and female

B

Looking at the layout tables above, we see that factor B is Drug. Our calculations gave a p value <0.05, meaning that factor B, drug, gave a significant difference. In other words, there is a difference in emotionality between subjects that received drug 1 as compared to subjects that received drug 2.

AxB

This is the interaction term. Definition of the interaction. What is interaction in factorial designs? Interaction is present if one level of one factor has a disproportionate effect on one level of the other factor.

2 x 3 factorial Analysis of

Variance ANOVA

The layout of a 2x3 factorial ANOVA

	B1	B2	B3
	A1B1 Subject 1 Subject 2 Subject 3 Subject 4 Subject 5	A1B2 Subject 6 Subject 7 Subject 8 Subject 9 Subject 10	A1B3 Subject 11 Subject 12 Subject 13 Subject 14 Subject 15
A1			
	A2B1 Subject 16 Subject 17 Subject 18 Subject 19 Subject 20	A2B2 Subject 21 Subject 22 Subject 23 Subject 24 Subject 25	A2B3 Subject 26 Subject 27 Subject 28 Subject 29 Subject 30
A2			

In this example of a factorial design, we have a 2x3 (we read this as "a two by three") factorial. Two by three, meaning two factors: A and B. "two" meaning two levels for factor A. "three" meaning three levels for B. In another case of a 3x2 factorial design we have two factors, A and B, factor A three levels, factor B two levels.

STATISTICS FOR COLLEGE STUDENTS AND RESEARCHERS

FORMAT OF 2x3 FACTORIAL ANOVA SUMMARY TABLE

Source	SS	df	MS	F	p
Between A					
Between B					
AxB (interaction)					
Within					
Total					

Interaction -factorial designs

Note the term "Interaction" in the ANOVA summary table of the factorial design What is interaction? The best way to grasp the concept of interaction is to graph it.

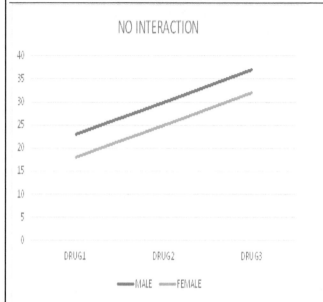

NO INTERACTION

STATISTICS FOR COLLEGE STUDENTS
AND RESEARCHERS

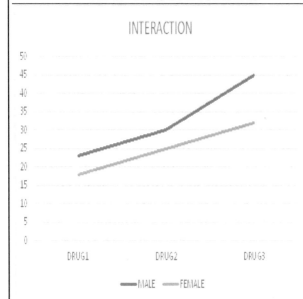

INTERACTION

STATISTICS FOR COLLEGE STUDENTS AND RESEARCHERS

ANOVA 2x3 factorial practice example

An experimenter wanted to test the effect of two drugs on the emotionality of male and female teenagers. He randomly selected 15 male and 15 female teenagers and randomly assigned them to 6 groups: Group 1, Group 2, Group 3, Group 4, Group 5, Group 6. five subjects in each group as shown in the following table.

STATISTICS FOR COLLEGE STUDENTS AND RESEARCHERS

	Drug 1 B1	Drug 2, B2	Drug 3, B3
Male A1	A1B1 Group1 Subject 1 Subject 2 Subject 3 Subject 4 Subject 5	A1B2 Group2 Subject 6 Subject 7 Subject 8 Subject 9 Subject 10	A1B3 Group3 Subject 11 Subject 12 Subject 13 Subject 14 Subject 15
Female A2	A2B1 Group3 Subject 16 Subject 17 Subject 18 Subject 19 Subject 20	A2B2 Group4 Subject 21 Subject 22 Subject 23 Subject 24 Subject 25	A2B3 Group2 Subject 26 Subject 27 Subject 28 Subject 29 Subject 30

The data are presented on the table below. The scores are the values recorded on a device measuring galvanic skin response, a measure of emotionality. Higher values indicate stronger emotion.

STATISTICS FOR COLLEGE STUDENTS
AND RESEARCHERS

STATISTICS FOR COLLEGE STUDENTS AND RESEARCHERS

	B1	B2	B3
	A1B1	A1B2	A1B3
	11	17	27
	11	18	25
A1	13	17	24
	12	16	26
	10	17	27
	A2B1	A2B2	A2B3
	15	20	30
	14	19	29
A2	14	18	29
	16	20	28
	15	18	31

.

2x3 FACTORIAL ANOVA SUMMARY TABLE

Source	SS	df	MS	F	p
Between A	67.5	1	67.5	62.31	<.0001
Between B	1088.07	2	544.04	502.19	<.0001
AxB (interaction)	3.8	2	1.9	1.75	0.1952
Within	26	24	1.08		
Total	1185.37	29			

After we calculate the F, we go to the F table to find the required F value for A, B, and AxB (interaction). Because,(remember?) the F ratio is A over within, B over within, AxB over within, we enter the F table with

STATISTICS FOR COLLEGE STUDENTS AND RESEARCHERS

df of A and df within , which is 1 and 24.
also B and df within, which is 2 and 24
and lastly AxB within., which is 2 and 24.
We first choose the F table at 0.05 level of
significance.

Factor A: The F at df 1 and 24 is 4.25. In the
summary table we see that the F for factor A
(rows) is 62.31. This is greater than 4.25, so
we conclude that here we have significance
at the 0.05 level of significance; we say
$p<0.05$, p less than 0.05. It has been
accepted among scientists that at the 0.05
level we are allowed to say that we have
significance, that the finding of our
experiment is reliable.

Next we look at factor B. We enter the F
table with df 2 and 24 and find F=3.50. This
is less than the F of our summary table
502.19, therefore we conclude that we have
significance at the 0.05 level. We formally
express this as follows: $p<0.05$.

Next we look at AxB. We enter the F table
with df 2 and 24 and find F=3.50.. This is
greater than the F at the summary table

value of 1.75 so we conclude that here we do not have significance. We formally express this as follows: p>0.05.

Step by step calculation of 2x3 ANOVA factorial

The goal of our calculations in ANOVA is to compute the F ratio, The F ratio is MS between over MS within. Mean Square is the mean of the squared deviations (differences) of each score from the mean. These are very simple calculations involving high school mathematics. Simple as they are, they are very important concepts in data analysis and beyond, that is science in general. You will never need to perform these calculations. There are many free Statistics calculators online. However, for the purpose of developing the concepts of ANOVA here are the steps:

1. Calculate the mean of each group.
2. Subtract each score from the mean.
3. Square each difference

4. Add these squared differences. font red
This is the Sum of Squares, the SS on the
ANOVA summary table.)
5. calculate the degrees of freedom df
(number of scores that went into the
calculation of the mean minus 1)
6 Divide the SS by the df. Voila! this the
MS.
7. The last step is to calculate the F. Divide
MS by the MS of the error term (which is
the MS within but may be something else
depending on which ANOVA design you
have.)

The F ratio, as all ratios, compares two
things. For example the ratio 8/4 compares 8
to 4 and finds that 8 is two times greater
than 4..

STATISTICS FOR COLLEGE STUDENTS AND RESEARCHERS

Understanding the 2x2 factorial ANOVA summary table

A
Looking at the layout tables above, we see that factor A is gender. Factor B is drug. Our calculations gave a p value <0.05 meaning that factor A, gender, gave a significant difference. In other words, there is a difference in emotionality between male and female

B
Looking at the layout tables above, we see that factor B is Drug. Our calculations gave a p value <0.05, meaning that factor B, drug, gave a significant difference. In other words, there is a difference in emotionality between subjects that received drug 1 as compared to subjects that received drug 2.

AxB
This is the interaction term. **Definition of the interaction. What is interaction in factorial designs?** Interaction is present if one level of one factor has a disproportionate effect on one level of the other factor.

STATISTICS FOR COLLEGE STUDENTS
AND RESEARCHERS

ANOVA mixed split plot

What is ANOVA mixed split plot design
ANOVA mixed designs, also called split
plot designs, are complex designs that
employ both independent and repeated
measures. The best way to explain this is
to present the layout of these
experimental designs.

TABLE SHOWING THE LAYOUT OF MIXED SPLIT-PLOT DESIGNS

Subjects	Drug 1	Drug 2
DEPRESSIVE		
1	50	68
2	55	63
3	56	65
4	50	67
5	56	69
6	54	68
SCHIZOPHRENIC		
7	99	122
8	100	125
9	110	130
10	90	135
11	105	140
12	115	131

Observe that there are two independent groups, depressive, and schizophrenic. Also observe that each subject of the depressive

and schizophrenic groups is repeatedly
tested, once with Drug 1, and later with
Drug 2. This is a repeated measures
arrangement So here we have a design in
which independent and repeated measures
are mixed. The name split plot comes from
the fact that this design is extensively used
in agricultural research.

**ANOVA mixed split plot designs -
formula**

As in all ANOVA, the formula for these
designs is:

$$F = \frac{MS_{between}}{MS_{within}}$$

We read this as follows: Mean square
between over mean square within. What is
mean square, you ask? It is the mean of
squares. What is squares, you ask. Squares is
the statistical term for squared deviations (of

squared differences) of each score X from the mean. What are the squared differences, you ask. Remember the formula for variance?

$$s^2 = \frac{\sum (X - \bar{X})^2}{n - 1}$$

Look at the numerator

$$\sum (X - \bar{X})^2$$

These are the squared differences summed. To complete our reasoning, we go back to where we started, the F formula, or F ratio, the formula for ANOVA. Why mean sums of squares? Simple because like all averages, we divide by the number of scores. If you are observant, you will notice that the F formula is a modified t formula.

FORMAT OF ANOVA MIXED SPIT PLOT SUMMARY TABLE

SOURCE	SS	df	MS	F	p
Between Independent					
	*	*	*	*	*
Error	*	*	*		
Total	*	*			
Between repeated measures					
A	*	*	*	*	*
AxB	*	*	*		*
Error	*	*	*		
Total		*			
TOTAL		*			

STATISTICS FOR COLLEGE STUDENTS AND RESEARCHERS

HOW TO CALCULATE df OF ANOVA MIXED SPIT PLOT SUMMARY TABLE

SOURCE	SS	df	MS	F	p
Between Independent					
B		number of independent groups minus 1	*	*	*
Error		total number of subjects minus the number of independent groups	*		
Total		total number of subjects minus 1			
Between repeated measures					
A	*	number of repetitions minus 1	*	*	*
AxB	*	df A x df B	*		*
Error	*	error between independent x number of repetitions	*		
Total		*			
TOTAL		total number of scores minus 1			

ANOVA mixed split plot practice example

An experimenter wanted to test drugs (factor A), Drug 1 (A1) and Drug 2 (A2) for their effect on serotonin level in the blood of patients (factor B) suffering from depression (B1) and schizophrenia (B2) . He randomly selected six patients suffering from depression and gave them Drug 1. He waited for one hour and then he measured the level of serotonin in nanograms per liter (ng/lt) of each subject. He recorded the data. One week later he gave these subjects Drug 2. He waited for one hour and measured the level of serotonin of each subject. He also randomly selected six patients suffering from schizophrenia and repeated the same experiment that he performed with the depressive patients. The data are presented in the table below.

STATISTICS FOR COLLEGE STUDENTS AND RESEARCHERS

ANOVA MIXED DESIGN

LAYOUT AND DATA

	Subjects	A1 Drug 1	A2 Drug 2
B1	DEPRESSIVE		
	1	50	68
	2	55	63
	3	56	65
	4	50	67
	5	56	69
	6	54	68
B2	SCHIZOPHRENIC		
	7	99	122
	8	100	125
	9	110	130
	10	90	135
	11	105	140
	12	115	131

STATISTICS FOR COLLEGE STUDENTS
AND RESEARCHERS

STATISTICS FOR COLLEGE STUDENTS AND RESEARCHERS

ANOVA MIXED SPIT PLOT SUMMARY TABLE

SOURCE	SS	df	MS	F	p
Between Independent					
B		1			
Error		10			
Total		11			
Between repeated measures					
A		1			
AxB		1			
Error		10			
Total		12			
TOTAL		23			

ANOVA repeated measures

ANOVA repeated measures - design

What are ANOVA repeated measures statistical designs?

ANOVA repeated measures statistical designs employ one group of subjects and give them the treatments of the experiments in succession. For example, a researcher that wants to test four different drugs for their possible effect on body temperature uses a single group of subjects rather than four groups. He will give them Drug 1, wait for a week, then give Drug 2, wait for a week, give Drug 3, wait for a week, then give Drug 4.The difference of repeated measures designs as compared to independent groups designs can be best illustrated by giving the layout of each.

The layout of independent groups ANOVA

Treatment 1	Treatment 2	Treatment 3	Treatment 4
Subject 1	Subject 6	Subject 11	Subject 16
Subject 2	Subject 7	Subject 12	Subject 17
Subject 3	Subject 8	Subject 13	Subject 18
Subject 4	Subject 9	Subject 14	Subject 19
Subject 5	Subject 10	Subject 15	Subject 20

The layout of repeated measures ANOVA

Subjects	Treatment 1	Treatment 2	Treatment 3	Treatment 4
1	X Subject 1	X Subject 1	X Subject 1	X Subject 1
2	X Subject 2	X Subject 2	X Subject 2	X Subject 2
3	X Subject 3	X Subject 3	X Subject 3	X Subject 3
4	X Subject 4	X Subject 4	X Subject 4	X Subject 4
5	X Subject 5	X Subject 5	X Subject 5	X Subject 5
6	X Subject 6	X Subject 6	X Subject 6	X Subject 6
7	X Subject 7	X Subject 7	X Subject 7	X Subject 7
8	X Subject 8	X Subject 8	X Subject 8	X Subject 8
9	X Subject 9	X Subject 9	X Subject 9	X Subject 9
10	X Subject 10	X Subject 10	X Subject 10	X Subject 10

STATISTICS FOR COLLEGE STUDENTS AND RESEARCHERS

FORMAT OF REPEATED MEASURES ANOVA SUMMARY TABLE

SOURCE1	SS	df	MS	F	p
Between Treatments					
Between Rows					
Error					
Totalr					

ANOVA repeated measures formula

The formula for Anova repeated measures experiments is the formula for variance The final step in the analysis of our data is the F ratio, which is variance of the data in particular ways.

$$F = \frac{MS_{between}}{MS_{within}}$$

ANOVA repeated measures- practice example

An experimenter wanted to test four new Drugs for their effect on body temperature. He randomly selected six subjects and gave them Drug 1. He waited for one hour and then he measured the temperature of each subject using a Celsius thermometer. He recorded the data. One week later he gave these subjects Drug 2. He waited for one hour and measured the temperature of each subject. A week later he gave these subjects Drug 3 One hour later he measured their temperature One week later he gave these same subjects Drug 4. He waited for one hour and then he measured their temperature. The data are presented in the table below.

STATISTICS FOR COLLEGE STUDENTS AND RESEARCHERS

Subjects	Treatment 1	Treatment 2	Treatment 3	Treatment 4
1	36.5	36.2	36.9	36.9
2	36.8	36.4	36.8	37.8
3	35.4	36.6	37.7	37.7
4	35.6	36.4	37.3	37.5
5	36.5	36.3	37.9	37.9
6	36.4	36.2	37.1	37.6

STATISTICS FOR COLLEGE STUDENTS AND RESEARCHERS

REPEATED MEASURES ANOVA SUMMARY TABLE

SOURCE	SS	df	MS	F	p
Between Treatments	8.2433	3	2.7478	15.84241	<0.05
Between Rows	3.2967	5	3.2967		
Error	2.6017	15	0.1734		
Totalr		23			

List of summary tables of ANOVA designs

Here is a list of summary tables of ANOVA designs: One-way, single factor ANOVA, 2x2 factorial design, 2x3 factorial, repeated measures, within design, mixed, split-plot ANOVA designs.

ONE-WAY SINGLE FACTOR ANOVA SUMMARY TABLE

Source	SS	df	MS	F	p
Between	1259	2	629.6	20.24	<0.0001
Within	373.2	12	31.10		
Total	1632	14			

2x2 FACTORIAL ANOVA SUMMARY TABLE

Source	SS	df	MS	F	p
Between A	36.45	1	36.45	41.66	<0.0001
Between B	120.05	1	120.05	137.2	<0.0001
AxB (interaction)	2.45	1	2.45	2.8	>0.95
Within	14	16	0.88		
Total	172.95	19			

STATISTICS FOR COLLEGE STUDENTS AND RESEARCHERS

REPEATED MEASURES ANOVA SUMMARY TABLE

SOURCE	SS	df	MS	F	p
Between Treatments	8.2433	3	2.7478	15.84241	<0.05
Between Rows	3.2967	20	3.2967		
Error	2.6017	15	0.1734		
Total					

STATISTICS FOR COLLEGE STUDENTS AND RESEARCHERS

FORMAT OF ANOVA MIXED SPIT PLOT SUMMARY TABLE

SOURCE	SS	df	MS	F	p
Between Independent					
B	*	*	*	*	*
Error	*	*	*		
Total	*	*			
Between repeated measures					
A	*	*	*	*	*
AxB	*	*	*		*
Error	*	*	*		
Total		*			
TOTAL		*			

Formulas for df in ANOVA

How to calculate

Here are the formulas for df in ANOVA. How to calculate df for all ANOVA designs

ONE-WAY ANOVA SUMMARY TABLE

Source	SS	df	MS	F	p
Between		number of independent groups minus 1			
Within		total number of scores minus number of independent groups			
Total		total number of scores minus 1			

STATISTICS FOR COLLEGE STUDENTS AND RESEARCHERS

2x2 FACTORIAL ANOVA SUMMARY TABLE

Source	SS	df	MS	F	p
Between A		number of independent groups of factor A minus 1			
Between B		number of independent groups of factor B minus 1			
AxB (interaction)		df A x df B			
Within		total number of scores minus number of groups			
Total		total number of scores minus 1			

STATISTICS FOR COLLEGE STUDENTS AND RESEARCHERS

ANOVA MIXED SPIT PLOT SUMMARY TABLE

SOURCE	SS	df	MS	F	p
Between Independent					
B		number of independent groups minus 1			
Error		total number of subjects minus the number of independent groups			
Total		total number of subjects minus 1			
Between repeated measures					
A		number of repetitions minus 1			

STATISTICS FOR COLLEGE STUDENTS AND RESEARCHERS

AxB	df A x df B		
Error	error between independent x number of repetitions		
Total			
TOTAL	total number of scores minus 1		

REPEATED MEASURES ANOVA SUMMARY TABLE

SOURCE	SS	df	MS	F	p
Between Treatments		number of treatments minus 1			
Between Rows		number of subjects minus 1			
Error		df between x df rows			
Total		total number of scores minus 1			

STATISTICS FOR COLLEGE STUDENTS
AND RESEARCHERS

STATISTICS FOR COLLEGE STUDENTS
AND RESEARCHERS

PART 2 LECTURE AND LAB

STATISTICS FOR COLLEGE STUDENTS AND RESEARCHERS

Introductory note

This part of the present book
is based on the lecture
notes and experiences that I
accumulated over many years
while teaching a
two-semester senior course in
experimental neuroscience.

The idea, encouragement, and
motivation to publish these lectures
comes from my students who have
been very successful in entering
graduate programs and holding
appointments in prestigious
schools such as Princeton,
Scripps Institute, MIT, Harvard,
Karolinska, Columbia and others.
Several of them did their doctoral
thesis with Nobel class research
teams and now hold faculty
appointments.

The most important part of a

scientific experiment is the mental
and practical activities before the
experiment has even started. When
the experiment is over, practically
all science-doing is over. At this
stage, statistical analysis, if
needed, will answer a simple
question: Is my finding reliable?
This simple and obvious fact is
often ignored in the frenzy of our
times.

If you plan to go to graduate school
and get a masters or Ph.D., you
have to know statistics. Knowing
statistics means that you
understand statistics.
Understanding statistics does not
mean using a wild array of
complex formulas. To the contrary,
formulas are often used in such a way
 that they blind you and prevent you
From understanding the concepts and
logic of statistics.

Analyzing your data is easy today.
Most statistics tests are on your

computer. They come with it when you buy it. There is also a plethora of web sites that offer you online data analysis. The difficulty is designing an experiment and in choosing the appropriate statistical test, and in justifying your analysis, e.g., in presenting your data in meetings, /and the oral defense of your thesis, masters or doctorate.

The goal of this book is to teach you the concepts of statistics by walking you through the evolution of statistical ideas in a simple and enjoyable manner.

I will guide you so that you understand the concepts of statistics as they emerged in the early history of this discipline. By understanding I mean that you grasp the concept, the procedure, or mechanism without words, at the gut level, as I say, and, surprise, no formulas! The few formulas (five simple formulas) that you will learn, simply

summarize what you already
know. You will be able to act out
these formulas in your mind,
without words. In short, I will teach
you with games and stories. It is
the game that is important, not the
formulas. If you know what you
are doing, you do not need a
recipe. The formulas, in a real
sense, are redundant.

After you read this book and digest
the concepts, you can teach fifth
graders Analysis of Variance by
devising games that they would
love to play.

On a more serious level, among
the gains of the trip we will take
together, will be the changes that
will take place in you, and
hopefully, you will become a
serious and successful scientist.

A promise.
Every single thing that I will ask
you to learn will be necessary for

the next step, and will be an important component in the edifice we will build. I will not ask you to learn anything that is not necessary for reaching our goal. All the things that you will learn are part of a pyramid, with Analysis of Variance at the top. You will not be asked to learn something just for the sake of learning it. We will build a pyramid and will use only the necessary materials, no ornaments, no things hanging out of the building.

Lecture 1 Numbers Quantities

Measurement

The four scales of measurement:
Nominal, ordinal, interval, ratio

The nominal scale of measurement

Drama
My kids my fingers

A family of early *homo sapiens* sitting
around a fire in a cave in Africa, devouring
their evening meal of a goat-like animal.
The kids are dancing and chasing each other.
The women chat and laugh aloud. The man
is staring into the dark opening of the cave
entrance. Now he raises his hands in front of
his eyes and with the index finger of his
right hand touches the fingers of his left

STATISTICS FOR COLLEGE STUDENTS AND RESEARCHERS

hand, fixing his eyes on his kids one by one. One kid, one finger. He repeats this with the index of his left hand. The next day he is out hunting again. Crouching in the bushes, he waits for the game to pass. Now he brings his hands in front of his eyes and looks at his fingers. He smiles. He knows how many children he has. At the gut level. No words. The dawn of a numbering system is in the air. Thousands of years later, the names of each finger will not be the names of a child, but symbols, words, that indicate the frequency of occurrence of children. Numbers. One, two, three, which are words, mind you. Thousands of years later, these words will be represented by written symbols: 1, 2, 3 and so on. Pretty primitive arithmetic, you will agree.

Drama
No-number numbers

Now let's get transported to a soccer football field in New York. You are watching the game with your friends. The truth is that you are not very fond of soccer, so you bring out your laptop computer and play around. Your friends are absorbed in the game, shouting, and jumping with excitement. In your boredom you ask: *Who is the guy with the number 11 on his shirt? He must be the best in the team. Poor number 3 he must be one of the worst players.* Your friends are looking at you irritated. Now you add up the numbers on the shirts of the football players. $1 + 2 + 3 + 4 + 5 + 6 + 7 + 8 + 9 + 10 + 11$. *Guys!* you shout, *the sum of the numbers on the football players is 66.* A while later you use your fancy laptop and calculate the standard deviation. *Guys!* You never finish your sentence, as your friends grab you and throw you out in the aisle.

STATISTICS FOR COLLEGE STUDENTS AND RESEARCHERS

You see that these numbers are strange numbers. They are more like words, *names*. You cannot add, them, subtract them, divide them. They do not express quantity.

These numbers are at the *nominal scale of measurement*. The only advantage of these numbers over names is this: they tell us how many elements we have. They refer to *non-orderable countables*.

Pretty primitive.

The ordinal scale of measurement

Drama

Who's bigger

Twenty first century Athens. Today the
Marathon race for women is taking
place. Before you leave home, you get a
glimpse of the athletes on TV at the start
line in Marathon. The end of the race is
Athens stadium in downtown Athens.
You get back home at dinner time and
find your family watching the news. The
three winners are proudly standing as
the national anthems play. *Great
athletes!* you say. Your family burst into
laughter. They are all laughing at you.
*Why are you laughing? I said something
wrong?* you say. *This was a great race,
especially in the smog of the city of
Athens.* They laugh at you even more.
Eventually your father explains to you.
The first athlete to terminate was indeed
great. She broke the world record.
However, the second to terminate broke
the world record in a negative sense.

She took so long to terminate the race
that no known race has recorded. The
smog made all athletes faint.

You see that this type of
measurement has an advantage
over the previous one (nominal). It
tells you what element is biggest,
second biggest, and so on. The
drawback is that it does not tell
you by how much the first differs
from the second and so on. You
did not know how many hours
slower was the second winner in
the Marathon race that we
considered above.

Numbers in this case are in the
ordinal scale of measurement.
Needless to say, you cannot add,
subtract, multiply or divide these
numbers. So, you cannot figure out
means or standard deviation. You
cannot run sophisticated statistical
analysis.

Primitive.

The interval scale of measurement

**Equal distance between
numbers**

Between 72 and 73 degrees
Fahrenheit there are subdivisions,
so you can express temperature
as 72.6 or 72.4. The distance
between 72 and 73 is considered
to be the same as the distance
between 73 and 74.

You see that this type of
measurement has an advantage
over the previous two. Most data
in the social science are of this
type of measures. Here you can
add, subtract, multiply, and,
practically speaking, divide,
However, there is one
disadvantage, if you want to be a
purist. Strictly speaking you cannot
divide. This will become clear in
the next type of measurement.

STATISTICS FOR COLLEGE STUDENTS AND RESEARCHERS

The ratio scale of measurement

My zero is not zero

In advanced sciences such as physics, measurement is a science in itself. When we say zero in Physics we mean absence of what we measure. And more than that.

Zero in physics must refer to the true state of affairs in the phenomenon we measure. Zero temperature in Physics means absence of molecular movement, since the definition of temperature is molecular movement of a substance. Temperature in Physics is measured with the Kelvin thermometer, which would show zero when there is total absence of molecular movement.

This type of measurement is like the interval type that we

considered above, but it is more
advanced, since here we can have
addition, subtraction,
multiplication, and division. This is
the *ratio scale of measurement.*

There are four types of
measurement, officially referred to
as *scales of measurement*:

nominal scale of measurement
ordinal scale of measurement
interval scale of measurement
ratio scale of measurement

What do you say?

*You told us that you will only cover
what is practically useful. What
use is all of this to me?*

Understanding the scales of
measurement is very useful. When
you are planning your experiment

you should spend some time considering what scale of measurement your data will be.

If you can choose interval or ratio scale of measurement, your experiment will be more profitable, and, also, you can run more sophisticated statistics.

When you have collected the data of your experiment, you want to analyze them using statistics. This is a big headache. You must choose the correct statistical test.

Grossly speaking, there are two books of statistical tests: *Parametric*, and *nonparametric*.

Here you are, after our first talk, you are in a position to choose one of the books for your data analysis. If your data are nominal or ordinal, you use nonparametric statistics, if your data are interval or ratio, you use parametric.

STATISTICS FOR COLLEGE STUDENTS AND RESEARCHERS

Lecture 2

Goddess Normal Curve

The normal distribution

The standard normal curve

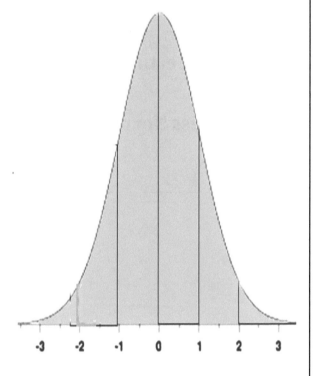

Standard deviation

You should bow and pray. This is

Goddess Normal Curve. The
mother of all. Elegant, but most
important, with hidden magic
qualities that you can profit from.

In our trips on the barren land of
Statistics, in times of despair, we
will ask her for help and
inspiration. Let me say this in
in other words. All the reasoning we
will engage in in this book, will be
while we stare at this goddess, as
we scratch our heads in search of
a solution.

Do not get discouraged by looking
at the graph above. Remember
fifth graders can understand this.

Ok, let's take a good look at it.
Notice that it looks like a Texas
hat. It is symmetrical, meaning
that, if you take a pair of scissors
and cut it in the middle, the two
parts are identical, or better, mirror
images.

It is perfect, isn't it?

Like a true goddess, the normal
curve does not exist in our
material world. What we see is
simply an imperfect reproduction
of it. The real normal curve exists
in our minds, it is a concept.
Mathematicians have produced a
formula which makes this graph
(See Appendix).

Now watch that in the middle of
the horizontal axis there is a 0.
On the right side of the midline 0
there are 2 vertical lines. There
are also 2 vertical lines on the left
of the midline 0. (I know you know
this without looking, since the two
parts are identical).

Drama
Working magic with a Goddess

Now get your fifth-grade pupil, Tom, and run
an experiment. Draw this curve on a card board. Take a pair of scissors and cut this curve out so that you really have a piece of cardboard that looks like a hat. Make sure this hat weighs 100 grams.
Now ask Tom to weigh the cardboard hat.

It is 100 grams, he says.

Ask Tom to cut the cardboard in the middle. Ask Tom to weigh the right side. He will refuse, he will say:

It is 50 grams, giggling.

Ask him to weigh the left side. He will laugh again. Now ask Tom to cut along the first vertical line on the right of the midline cut. He does and holds the strip of cardboard in his hands. Ask him to guess its weight. His pride is deflated, he does not know. You do not know either. Weigh this strip, you will

STATISTICS FOR COLLEGE STUDENTS AND RESEARCHERS

find that it weighs 34 grams.
Ask Tom to cut along the first vertical line
on the left half of the hat and guess its
weight.

He will refuse.

I*t is 34 grams*, he will say.

Next give Tom a new cardboard cutout
of the normal curve, and ask him to cut
along the second vertical line on the
right side of the midline, and cut
along the second vertical line on the left
of the midline on the left side.

The standard normal curve

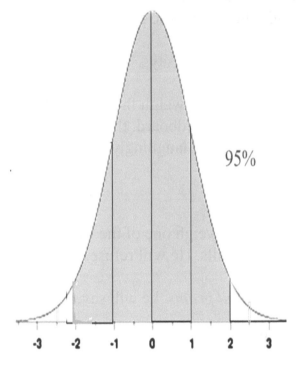

95%

Standard deviation

He holds three pieces now, the big middle
part (gray), and the two, tiny, pointed parts
(white), the "tails" of the curve. Ask Tom to
weigh the big middle part. He does.

It is 95 grams, he says.

Now ask him to weigh the two small
pieces of the cardboard, the "tails". He
will refuse, and laughingly he will say

5 grams.

Ask him to weigh one of the small
pieces, or tails. He will refuse.

2 and a half grams, he will say.

Child's play, you agree?

If you were to ask a
mathematician to do this
experiment for you, he would
laugh at you right away.
Mathematicians can calculate this
from the formula that generates
the normal curve. I will show you

that formula later on.

The numbered points of the vertical lines, 3 on each side of the midline, they call "standard deviations". Standard deviation +1, standard deviation +2, standard deviation +3 on the right side, and standard deviation -1, standard deviation -2, standard deviation -3 on the left side.

We do not have to worry about this. What we should always remember is that that if we cut the cardboard model of the normal distribution along the second vertical line to the right and left of the midline (that is at standard deviations +2 and -2), the bigger piece weighs approximately 95 grams, and the two small pieces, the "tails" weigh approximately 5 grams.

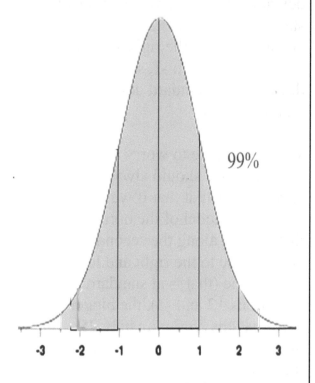

The standard normal curve

99%

Standard deviation

STATISTICS FOR COLLEGE STUDENTS
AND RESEARCHERS

Now if we cut at -2.5 and at +3.5. The middle (gray)
piece weighs approximately 99 grams, while the two outwards
noses or tails of the curve (white) weigh approximately 1 gram, each 0.5 grams.

In other words, approximately 99% of the cardboard weight is between standard deviation +2.5 and -2.5, and 1% of the cardboard weight is beyond standard deviation +2.5 and -2.5 (white). These are approximate values.

It is important that you remember this.

Approximately, you say. *What are the exact values?*

STATISTICS FOR COLLEGE STUDENTS
AND RESEARCHERS

Standard deviation 1.96
Percent of curve 95%

Standard deviation 2.56
Percent of curve 99%

It is important that you remember
this!

The standard normal curve

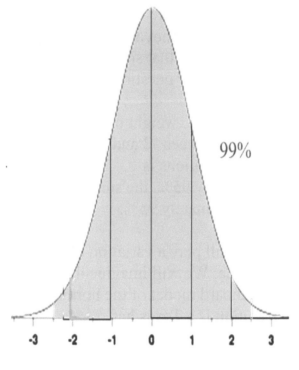

99%

Standard deviation

You can see this on the curve. The gray part of the curve is between -2.56 and +2.56, that is just before 3.

STATISTICS FOR COLLEGE STUDENTS AND RESEARCHERS

Let me ask you something. What is the surface area of the cardboard, between standard deviation -2 and +2? Amazingly, most students cannot answer this question. I know that some of you see this as a silly question.

Of course, if the weight of the cardboard between -2 and +2 standard deviations is approximately 95%, the surface is also approximately 95%.

Now we will play a variation of the same game. We will imagine that the cardboard model of the normal distribution is a Texas hat.

We stand at a corner in downtown Houston and ask a man passing by to, please, allow us to measure his height. We write his height on a small piece of paper, and throw it in the hat, and of course we also type it in a laptop computer. After we measure the heights of 1000

men, we get into the boring task of
arranging the small pieces of
paper in the hat, stacking them up.
The smallest numbers go to the
extreme left, and the large
numbers to the extreme right, and
the rest, the middle of the road
values, in between. As you would
expect, there will be very few men
that are very short. Most men will
be around a middle value, the
average, and again, very few men
will be extremely tall. Look at the
normal distribution. As we move
from left to right the height of the
curve increases, it reaches a peak
exactly in the midline, and
decreases again on the right side.
You see that the height of the
curve indicates *frequency* (how
many times, a given height
occurs).

Below the tallest point of the curve
is the mean, the average. This, as
you can easily see is also the
most frequent score, the *mode*,

that is the most fashionable score.

The scores (the small pieces of paper with the heights of Texans) between standard deviations +2 and -2 represent approximately 95% of the total number of scores we put into the hat. The scores between standard deviation +3 and -3 represent 99% of the scores. Again, these are approximate values.

Let us pause for a moment and see where we are and what we are doing.

We said that the normal curve is a kind of goddess that helps us reason in statistical problems. We saw some of its characteristics and saw that the markings of standard deviation help us calculate the percentage of the weight, the surface area, or the frequency of scores of this curve.

STATISTICS FOR COLLEGE STUDENTS
AND RESEARCHERS

What do you say?

*You told us that we will understand
perfectly every step and every
concept as we go along*, you say.
*I do not understand what standard
deviation is.*

Ok. We will develop the concept of
standard deviation right away.

Lecture 3

Variance and standard

deviation

STATISTICS FOR COLLEGE STUDENTS
AND RESEARCHERS

Drama
Mathematical sweat

Susan Bolles is a new professor of
Psychology at Goatshead College.
Her chairman, sorry, chairperson, Dr.
Alexa Terrorvski, assigned her the
introductory psychology class of
1000 students. The first midterm
exam has just taken place. There
were 100 questions, 1 point each.
The exam papers were
computer-graded, all 1000 of them.
Dr. Terrorvski wants to know how
the class did, so she asks Susan.
Susan says that the mean (the
average) was 60.

Dr. Terrorvski wants to know more,
how many people scored close to
100, and how many people scored
close to zero. Susan walks up to the
pile of exam sheets and starts
reading the scores: *48, 30, 70, 99,
53 ......* Papers are spread out from
the middle point, the average.
Realizing that this would take a good part

— 146 —

STATISTICS FOR COLLEGE STUDENTS
AND RESEARCHERS

of the day, Dr. Terrorvski shouts out:

There must be a better way!
I will tell you what. Take this pile out to the
stadium, put it down in the middle of the
stadium. Mark this point 60 (your average
score). Take a step and mark this point 61.
Another step, mark this 62, all the way to
100. Return to mark 60 and take a step in
the opposite direction. Mark this point
59. Take another step, and mark this 58,
repeat all the way to mark 0. Now return to
your pile of exam sheets and pick up an
exam sheet. Read the score and walk to the
point it corresponds to on the markings you
made. I will return in an hour to see how
the exam went.

When Dr. Terrorvski returns she finds
Susan drenched in sweat and panting
vigorously. There is a long line of white
sheets of paper on both sides of the
point that marks 60, the average.
Susan picks up another exam sheet
which had the score of 3 and begins
walking. 59. 58. 57

STATISTICS FOR COLLEGE STUDENTS AND RESEARCHERS

Enough! Terrorvski shouts. *This is a mess. Look at how many papers are spread out away from the mean, students have scored low scores, all the way down to zero. So many scores, so many students are very far from 60, the mean. There is a big distance of many scores from the mean. You need to be more effective in teaching your students, even the weak ones,* Dr. Terrorvski said, and marched out of the stadium.

Susan went to her office and tried to get a better picture of the situation. Rather than walking away from the point of the mean, she calculated the distance of each score from the mean. Score 40. Distance from the mean -20. Score 65. Distance from the mean +5. And so on. At the end she added up all these distances and she found the total distance. That was the distance she had to walk in the stadium!

STATISTICS FOR COLLEGE STUDENTS AND RESEARCHERS

In the second midterm, the mean
was again 60. This time she did
not go out in the stadium. She
simply found out the distance of
each score from the mean. She
added up all these distances
and was pleased to see that the
total distance was very small.
Surely, Dr. Terrorvski would not
yell at her this time. Students
scored close to the mean, there
were very few low scores. The
scores this time were not spread
out all over the place away from
the mean.

Let's see what Susan did. She
calculated the average, the mean.
As even fifth grader Tom knows,
we find the mean by adding up all
scores, and divide by how many
scores went into the calculation.

The formula for this is

STATISTICS FOR COLLEGE STUDENTS
AND RESEARCHERS

$$\overline{X} = \frac{\sum X}{n}$$

We read this as follows: X bar, equals the sum of X divided by n.

X bar is the symbol for the mean. Σ is the symbol for addition, sum. X is the symbol for score. n is the symbol for how many scores.

After calculating the mean, Susan. calculated the distance (the deviation) of each score from the mean. In doing this she calculated the total distance of all scores from the mean. That is, she calculated a measure of the spread, or dispersion of scores around the mean. That is a measure of variation or variance of scores.

The symbol for variance is s^2. The formula for variance is

STATISTICS FOR COLLEGE STUDENTS AND RESEARCHERS

$$s^2 = \frac{\sum (X - \bar{X})^2}{n - 1}$$

We read this as follows:
Variance equals the sum of squared deviations of each score from the mean, divided by how many scores went into the calculation.

Why squared? Why square the deviation, you say.

The sum of deviations from the mean *always*, in all cases, equals 0. That is why we square each deviation to prevent this. You should know that in all sciences, for the purpose of meaningful analysis, we may transform our data by squaring them, or expressing them as logarithms, and so on. This does not change the relation of scores amongst themselves.

STATISTICS FOR COLLEGE STUDENTS
AND RESEARCHERS

Why divide by n?

You understand that if in one case
we have large scores, and in
another small scores, the sum of
the deviations from the mean will
be large in the first instance, and
small in the second instance. If we
want to compare the spread of the
scores in the two instances, we
have to average each of these
sums of deviations. I hope you
understand this.

For example, in order to compare
the income of New Yorkers to
that of Chicagoans, we must
average the total income of New
Yorkers and Chicagoans.
The numerator of this formula

$$\sum(X - \overline{X})^2$$

is the sum of the difference of
each score squared, or raised to
the second power. More formally,
we say the numerator of the variance
formula is the sum of squared
deviations of each score from the
mean, squared. In statistical jargon
we say:

Sum of squares, or SS.

> The numerator of the variance
> formula is the
> **Sum of Squares,**
> or **SS**

The denominator is the n, i.e., the
number of scores we have in this
case. Dividing by how many
scores we have the mean or
average.

So, the variance formula is the
average of the sum of squared
deviations, or, in statistical jargon,
the mean squares or MS, for
short.

STATISTICS FOR COLLEGE STUDENTS
AND RESEARCHERS

> Variance is also called
> ***mean squares***
> or
> ***MS***

What is standard deviation? you
say.

To calculate the standard deviation
we take the square root of
variance. Simple.

You do not need to know how to
calculate the square root of a
number. Not in the age of
computers. Anyone can learn to
do simple arithmetic. The
challenge is to understand
concepts of statistical and
mathematical operations.

The formula for standard deviation
is:

$$s = \sqrt{\frac{\sum(X - \overline{X})^2}{n - 1}}$$

Do not worry about the -1 in the denominator. The n changes depending on whether we deal with samples or an entire population. Remember our goal here is to understand the concepts of statistics and want to avoid getting stuck in compulsive swamps.

We use n-1 when we work with samples. We N without -1 when we refer to population.

Now that we have removed the mystery of standard deviation of the normal distribution, we return to it.

Remember this is not just a curve, it is Goddess Normal Curve. Glory to NC in the highest!

STATISTICS FOR COLLEGE STUDENTS AND RESEARCHERS

Lecture 4

The uses of the normal

distribution

STATISTICS FOR COLLEGE STUDENTS AND RESEARCHERS

You ask:

*Why learn all these things about
the normal curve? What is the use
of all of this*?

The use of all of this is necessary,
I say.

The normal curve (the *standard normal
curve*) is a mathematical, perfect curve,
With magic qualities and powers.
Understanding the normal curve is
necessary, if we wish to
understand statistics from simple
t-tests to complex Analysis of
Variance (ANOVA).

STATISTICS FOR COLLEGE STUDENTS AND RESEARCHERS

The normal curve is used in four instances:

1. To describe, to organize data.

2. To make statements regarding probabilities as to the occurrence of a particular score, as in games of chance.

3. To make statements regarding the reliability of a single mean

4. To make statements regarding the reliability of the difference between two means.

Understanding the concepts in number 4 above is the basis for understanding the concepts of all statistical tests. Also, as we said before, there is a continuity in the process of our understanding of

— 158 —

statistics.

It is like a fairy tale. You must know the full story, starting from the beginning and step by step reach the end, in order to make sense. So keep alert!

STATISTICS FOR COLLEGE STUDENTS AND RESEARCHERS

Normal distribution,
Use number 1

To describe, to organize data

Michelangelo, Sistine Chapel

Point of contact.
God's hand makes contact with the hand of
Man. Genesis. Magic moment. A whole
world begins here. The divine, the
immaterial, the perfect makes contact with
the earthly, imperfect, and imparts to it
some of the harmony of the spiritual, perfect
world.

Drama
Where does Basita fall?

Susan, our psychology professor,
decided to take a personal interest in the
learning of her students, and called
those scoring very low to her office.
Among those she called was Basita.

*The bottom line of this is that you should
quit college immediately. You are the
bottom of the bottommost. You will
never be able to compete with other
college students. Find a job in a diner, in
a farm, anywhere, but do not waste your
time at college,* she said to Basita.

The next day, Basita and her mother,
Mrs. Thinlips, an accountant by
profession, marched into Susan's office.

*I have already talked to your chairperson
about this. I demand that you explain to
me the basis of your criticism and absurd
advice to my daughter. You traumatized
her, in effect telling her that she is an*

idiot. You will hear from my lawyer. For now I want an explanation.

My daughter scored 45. The mean was 60. Forty-five is close to the mean, only 15 points below. Forty-five means that Basita knows almost half of what you expect her to know. Your telling my daughter to quit college is most unwarranted. I demand an explanation! Mrs. Thinlips said, banging her fist on the Susan's desk.

Help, Susan said to herself, *Goddess Normal Curve, help*. She brings out a sizable cardboard model of the goddess and bows.

Mrs., Thinlips, she said. *The mean of the scores in Basita's class was indeed 60, and the standard deviation was 5. Here is the computer analysis.*

Now we place 60 on the mean (0 standard deviation), that is in the middle of the curve.

STATISTICS FOR COLLEGE STUDENTS AND RESEARCHERS

Flash, thunder, tempest winds, Michelangelo hovers over the cardboard model! Angels and ministers of heaven and hell! Point of contact of the spiritual with the material! A new science is born. Statistics. All else is humble things after the cosmogony of this moment of Genesis. All subsequent statistical tests bow to this archetypal creation.

We place 60 on the mean, that is in the middle of the curve, Susan continues. *Now we move down to standard deviation -1, to the first vertical line on the left of the midline. This means that at this point we have score 55. Now we move down one more standard deviation, standard deviation -2. Here we have score 50. Finally, we move down one more standard deviation, standard deviation -3. Here we have score 45. This is Basita's score. The percentage of scores above this point is 99.5%. That is one student out of 200 scored 45 or lower. Since we have 1000 students in this class, no more than 5 students scored the same or lower than Basita. Imagine a line of 1000 students, a*

*small town, and your daughter standing at
the very end!* Susan said, with a malicious
smile on her face.
Mrs. Thinlips or Basita have not been seen
on the campus ever since.

Back to our task to understand the
normal distribution, to understand
it our way, a gut-level
understanding.

In doing science we have two
domains, two worlds. The
empirical domain, the mud and
flesh domain, and the *formal
domain*, the domain of
abstractions, ideas, logic and
mathematics. The empirical
domain is our sense world, and
the data we get by running
experiments in it.

The formal domain is the world of
thought and mathematics.
Sciences progress by
superimposing perfect models of
mathematics on the imperfect,

variable, messy world of matter.
When we do that, we immediately
see things that we could not see
by looking only at the data we
have collected from observations
in the material world.

Newton succeeded in creating a
revolution in Physics by first
creating a calculus, which he
superimposed on nature. Galileo
Galilei, the man who started
science as we know it today, said
that the language of nature is
mathematics.

A most important note in Basita's
story:

What if Basita's score was not 45
but it was 43? How would we find
where it falls on the normal curve?
There is a formula called the z
formula. Here it is:

$$z = \frac{(X - \overline{X})}{s}$$

Let's try it.

Score 43 minus the mean, which is 60, equals -17. Now if we divide -17 by the standard deviation which is 5 here, we get a z of -3.4. That makes sense. Basita's score of 45 fell exactly on standard deviation -3, as we saw. A score of 43 will be even more to the left of the curve.

I do not want to close this talk. I want to play some triumphant march, Beethoven's Eroica perhaps. Look at this formula. Play with it, do things with it. Digest what we do with it. Let's dramatize this.

$$z = \frac{(X - \overline{X})}{s}$$

Drama

An archetypal ceremony

I pick a score, and wave it in the
air. Then I wear my glasses and
stick my nose on the normal
curve, running up and down the
line with standard deviations on
it, I mumble:

*Where does this score fall? Where
does this score fall?*

I then use the z formula and find
where exactly my score falls.

This is an archetypal ceremony.
Remember it. We will act it out
again in the future.

STATISTICS FOR COLLEGE STUDENTS AND RESEARCHERS

Normal distribution, use number 2

Making statements of probability, betting

Drama

Money in a Texas hat

After taking my course, Nick, an entrepreneurial mind, decided to go into business. He went south to Houston Texas, and planned a betting business without any substantial investment. Just an antique Texas Instruments calculator. For two months he stood at a corner in downtown Houston asking every man that appeared around the corner:

Excuse me, sir, would you mind if I measure how tall you are? I am running my thesis and need data.

He carefully recorded the data. At the end of the two months he had measured the heights of 4000 men. Now he punched his data into the calculator and computed the mean and the standard deviation.
The mean was 170 cm, that is 1 meter and 70 centimeters. The

standard deviation was 10.

The next morning, he puts on his brightest face, and stands at the same corner in downtown Houston. Time to make money.

Excuse me sir, I bet $1000.00 that the first man that will appear around the corner will be between 1 meter 50 centimeters, and 1 meter 90 centimeters tall.

Not all passersby pay attention to him but a few do.

Oh Yeah? How do you know, buddy? You think you are smart, ah? Here is $1000. Show me yours.

Tom puts down his $1000. Here he comes, first man appears around the corner. He agrees to be measured. His height is 170. Nick wins. Nick will make several thousand dollars on his first day. He loses a few times but 95% of the time he wins.

Let's see his reasoning.

He followed my example of Basita's story. He placed the mean of the heights,170 cm, (the one that he computed from his data) on the middle of the normal curve. Now he reasoned that since the standard deviation of his data was 10, at standard deviation -1 score 160 exists, at standard deviation -2 score 150 exists, and at standard deviation -3 score 140 exists.

Similarly, on the right side of the curve, score 180 is at standard deviation +1, score 190 is at standard deviation +2, and score 200 is at standard deviation +3.

One more example:

Mean 20
Standard deviation 3

STATISTICS FOR COLLEGE STUDENTS
AND RESEARCHERS

What standard deviation score 26 lies at?

Answer: Score 26 lies at standard deviation +2

At standard deviation +1 we have score 23, i.e., 20+3

At standard deviation +2 we have score 26, i.e., 20+3+3

At standard deviation +3 we have score 29, i.e., 20+3+3+3

At standard deviation -1 we have score 17, i.e., 20-3

At standard deviation -2 we have score 14, i.e., 20-3-3

At standard deviation -3 we have score 11, i.e., 20-3-3-3

STATISTICS FOR COLLEGE STUDENTS AND RESEARCHERS

Normal distribution
Use number 3

To make statements
regarding the reliability of a
single mean

Drama

A Cap for Wisconsin Farmers

Mike got his degree in Psychology from UW Madison. Given the large number of psychology graduates and also his doubts regarding his suitability for psychology practice, he found a job as a consultant with the State of Wisconsin. Psychologists, you should know, learn a lot of statistics. Around the middle of last November, his boss walked into his office and said:

Mike, I have a job for you. The governor has decided to give a present to all farmers in the State of Wisconsin because they are very angry with the new taxes. The gift will be a woolen cap. We want to know the size of the cap. If we can find the average head size of Wisconsin farmers, we can give the order to a factory in Milwaukee to make the caps. They are woolen so they naturally stretch. If we know the average head size we will be ok. Since we only have one month to complete this project, I expect you to report to me with a plan and budget tomorrow.

Early the next morning Mike walked into his boss's office and handed him the proposal. Three hundred personnel to cover the entire state, to locate *every* farmer, in one weak. Fifty 4x4 Jeeps to safely travel to even the remotest towns. One small aircraft to land in the northern towns in case of snow. Three hundred laptops. Ten German Shepherds to smell the bears up and around Wausau. Budget. $30,000.00.

His boss looked at Mike for 20 seconds speechless. Then, in a completely unemotional voice, he said:

Mike, in the State of Wisconsin we are very careful with our money. No way. Find a less expensive way by tomorrow.

Mike began to fear for his job. All day in his office, all night in his home, he scratched his head, drank a lot of coffee, and prayed to Goddess Normal Curve.

STATISTICS FOR COLLEGE STUDENTS AND RESEARCHERS

*I am not allowed to measure **all** farmer heads. That is too expensive. I can, perhaps, still find a way to use the normal curve. If I can come up with a mean that has a strong probability to be close to the real mean... If I take measures of the heads of many farmers and compute the mean.... Can I be sure that this is close to real mean? If not, I will lose my job. So, what if I go out a second time and repeat the data collection, just to make sure that this mean was not a mean that I got by chance but it was a mean close to the real mean. Ah, that might be it! I go out several times and each time I compute the mean. In the end I graph these means (as though they were scores).*

Then I use the normal curve to reason in some way. How? Let me see... The normal curve would be graphing means. So, the mean would be the mean of the means. Can I play the game of Nick? He was making probability statements, predictions, regarding the occurrence of scores, using the standard deviation of the

STATISTICS FOR COLLEGE STUDENTS AND RESEARCHERS

scores. Ah! I can use the standard deviation of the means. Then I can reason, like Nick, that a mean close to the mean of means, that is between standard deviation -2 and +2 would have a high probability of occurrence. That's it!

He prepares the budget, and early in the morning he busts into his boss's office.

It will cost us $10,000, he says.
Good idea, but too expensive.
Tomorrow is the last day, boss says, and with the palm of his hand he points at the door.

Three in the morning, Mike is on his knees in front of Goddess Normal Curve, buried in statistics books and statistics journals, and notes from his stat class. Suddenly he comes across an article in a journal which claims that you can calculate an estimate of the standard deviation of the normal curve that would be graphing means.

STATISTICS FOR COLLEGE STUDENTS AND RESEARCHERS

...that would be graphing means... Would be..., he repeats this several times.

Would be, because this curve has only one mean. Let me say it in another way. You go out and you collect data from a large sample. You can calculate an estimate of the standard deviation of the curve that would be graphing the means of samples that you would be getting if you were allowed to collect several samples.

We*ird...,* Mike mumbles. *What good is it? I want to be able to collect one sample, calculate the mean, and tell my boss that we can trust this mean as being close to the real head size of Wisconsin farmers, that it is reliable. What good is computing an estimate of the standard deviation of a curve and not know much else about this curve...*

The traffic noise picks up, it is six o'clock in the morning. Another look at the Goddess, and a supplication for inspiration.

— 179 —

STATISTICS FOR COLLEGE STUDENTS
AND RESEARCHERS

All I know is what Nick did, Mike says. *He placed the mean of his data on the normal curve mean (middle). Unfortunately, I do not have the mean of the means, since I am allowed to take only one mean. Let me place the letters TM in the middle of the normal curve, TM for True Mean. TM will remain forever unknown. Pretty spooky. But I can place the standard deviation of this "I-would-be-getting" curve, an estimate of the standard deviation, to be exact.*

Ok, then what.

Weird things happen to people under stress and in despair. Some people hear voices, others are visited by angels, others write poetry…

Got it! he suddenly exclaims, raises the normal curve over his head, and dances a cannibal dance around his desk.

Eight in the morning he rushes into his Boss's office.

STATISTICS FOR COLLEGE STUDENTS
AND RESEARCHERS

One day, one sample, one mean, one thousand dollars! he yelps.

His boss pretends he is not listening.

I will go out, one day, collect many head size scores, calculate this mean. Next, I will compute an estimate of the standard deviation of this curve that you did not allow me to get the data for. I will then run down two standard deviations from the middle of the curve (-2 to +2).

Mike pauses to get some feedback from his boss. Stone silence.

Grant me this, Mike continues in a loud voice. *This curve would be graphing means, right? My one mean is one of these means, right?*

That is absolutely correct, and also tautologous, boss says, and looks at Mike with contempt.

What is the chance that this mean would be one of the 95 percent of the means? Mike asks.

It's highly probable, almost certain,
boss replies.

*Then the problem boils down to the
size of the standard deviation of
this curve, i.e., the estimate that we
will compute. If the standard
deviation is large, then we would
run the risk of producing caps that
are ridiculously large or small for
the heads of Wisconsin farmers. If
the standard deviation is small, our
mean would almost certainly be
close to the true mean, and we are
in business.*

Mike carried out this project
successfully without any problems,
except that he was chased by a
playful bear at *Wausau* up north.

STATISTICS FOR COLLEGE STUDENTS AND RESEARCHERS

The formula for the calculation of the estimate of the standard deviation of the curve that we would be getting if we were allowed to get many samples, but are allowed only to take one sample, and so have only one mean, is:

$$SEM = \frac{s}{\sqrt{n}}$$

We read this as follows: standard error of the mean equals the standard deviation (of the data from our one sample), divided by the square root of the number of data that go into the calculation, i.e., the n. Yes, you guess right, the official name for the estimate of the standard deviation of the curve that would be graphing means is called *standard error of the mean.*

STATISTICS FOR COLLEGE STUDENTS AND RESEARCHERS

Normal distribution
Use number 4

To make statements
regarding the reliability of
the difference between two means

STATISTICS FOR COLLEGE STUDENTS AND RESEARCHERS

A psychologist at the University of California published a study in which she claimed that college students who prefer Polish sausage react faster as compared to college students who eat plain hotdogs. She measured the time it takes to respond when a stimulus, a buzzer, is presented.

Here is a summary of the data:

Reaction Time ms

	Polish Sausage	Hotdog
Mean	210	215
Standard deviation	20	25
	200	200

The difference between the two means is 5 milliseconds. The Polish sausage group responds in

less time, that is this group is
faster. However, a question pops
up: Is this difference reliable?
Which means, will we find this
difference, if we run the
experiment again, or this
difference was perhaps found by
chance.

We can use the normal distribution
to solve this problem. However, it
is the almost universal practice in
many sciences to use the t-test,
the so-called *Student's t-test*. The
t-test was created by William
Sealy Gosset.

STATISTICS FOR COLLEGE STUDENTS
AND RESEARCHERS

Lecture 5

The t-test

STATISTICS FOR COLLEGE STUDENTS
AND RESEARCHERS

William Sealy Gosset
(June 13, 1876–October 16, 1937)
Wikipedia Aug, 2014 PD

STATISTICS FOR COLLEGE STUDENTS AND RESEARCHERS

William Sealy Gosset published the t-test under the pen name *Student*. We refer to the distribution of this test as the *t-distribution*. The t-test is *a test of inference*, i.e., it allows us to infer on the basis of our data, whether the difference between two means is reliable or, as we say, *significant*.

In what follows, we will first try to develop the concepts needed for understanding the logic and the operations involved in the t-test.

We will talk about this and that and the other. Be patient. Then we will go over an example of the t-test.

**Developing the concepts in the
t-test**

As is the case with all parametric
tests that we will cover in this
book, the t-test analysis is based
on variance.

In experiments in which we have
two groups we analyze our data by
using the t-test. There are two
types of t-tests. The *t-test for
independent samples* (groups),
and the other for dependent or
paired samples. Here we will
consider independent samples.

What are independent samples?
you say.

Ok. We will make a small
parenthesis in order to develop the
concept of independence.

DramaApple-pie IQ

A psychologist has a sneaky suspicion that the type of apple pie has an effect on intelligence. She randomly selected 20 students and randomly assigned them to two groups. Group 1, golden delicious apple pie, Group 2, red delicious apple pie. John Gluck was assigned in Group 1, and his friend Paul Crust was assigned to Group 2. The psychologist proceeded with giving these subjects a pound of apple pie to eat. Subsequently she tested their intelligence. Each subject was allowed to see their intelligence score. There were 20 intelligence scores, one for each subject. These groups are independent as you see. She analyzed her data by using a t-test for independent groups in order to see if there was a significant difference in intelligence in the two groups.

Note: An unexpected event occurred during the running of the experiment. One of the subjects in Group 2 did not show up on time so the experiment was delayed for a few minutes. John Gluck, who, as you remember, was in Group 1, offered to participate in Group 2, in addition to his participation in Group 1. The experimenter did not allow this. Had she allowed John Gluck to be a subject in both groups, she would have violated the rule of independence, and she would not have been able to analyze her data by using the t-test for independent samples.

STATISTICS FOR COLLEGE STUDENTS AND RESEARCHERS

The formula for the t-test is:

$$t = \frac{\overline{X_1} - \overline{X_2}}{\sqrt{\dfrac{s_1^{\,2}}{n_1}} + \sqrt{\dfrac{s_2^{\,2}}{n_2}}}$$

We read this as follows:

T equals mean 1 minus mean 2 divided by the square root of the variance of group 1 and group 2 divided by the number of scores that went into the calculation of the variance.

Faithful to our goal we must understand the concepts in the t-test.

First look at the numerator. Mean 1 minus mean 2, that is the difference of the two means.

Next look at the denominator.
The square root of the variance
is the standard deviation.
This looks like the z formula that
 we considered above. Here it is again:

$$z = \frac{(X - \overline{X})}{s}$$

Yes, you say, *but the numerator of
the z formula is score minus the
mean. The numerator of the t-test
formula is mean 1 minus mean 2.
Where is the mean? They are not
the same,* you say.

They are the same, I say. Mean 1
minus mean 2 is the difference
between the two means. Gosset
treats this difference as a score.

Yes, you say, *but then where is*

the mean in the t-formula?

The mean is there! I say.

It is there but you do not see it. It
is 0. The mean is zero.

The mean is zero!

STATISTICS FOR COLLEGE STUDENTS AND RESEARCHERS

Let the drums thunder at this
point. Let the bugles sound in the
four corners of the world!

The normal (t-) distribution with 0
in the middle. In other words, a
curve with a mean of 0.

 A most important point in the history of
statistics.

Let us call this curve the
curve of no difference.

*I do not understand the t formula
at the gut level,* you say.

Watch the ritual dance with the
t-formula.

Drama
An archetypal ceremony II

I have a difference between
the two means. I hold this
difference up, wave it in the
air, *I baptize it score*. Then I
wear my glasses and stick my
nose on the t curve, running
up and down the line with
standard deviations on it, and
mumble: *where does this
score fall? Where does this
score fall?*

I then use the z formula -
oops, the t-formula - and
find where exactly our score -
oops, our difference - falls.

This is an archetypal ceremony.
Remember? Amazing, isn't it? The
t-formula is actually the z formula!
I promised you that you do not
need the mind-boggling array of
fear inspiring formulas. Hang on.

STATISTICS FOR COLLEGE STUDENTS AND RESEARCHERS

Here is more of the story of the t distribution. The motive in Gosset's mind was to modify the normal curve so that it could safely be used for small samples. He decided to make it difficult for researchers to find significance (i.e., to decide whether the difference between our two means is reliable) when the samples are small. The curve he created is a normal curve with some intriguing qualities. The noses, or tails of the curve lift up as the sample size decreases. The tails of the curve lift up. You can see that in the graph that follows.

The shorter (lower) curve corresponds to the smaller sample.

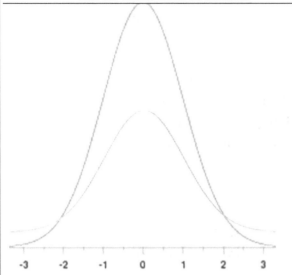

What an ingenious idea!

Some of you, few, very few,
already see what this means. It
means that it becomes more
difficult for you to find significance
because the percentage of the
curve increases in the tails so that
the magic standard deviation of
1.96 becomes larger, which in turn
makes it difficult for you to find
significance, that is to have a

"real" effect, a "true" finding so that
you can publish your experiment.

Let's finish this story of the t-test,
a statistical test that is used so
frequently in labs across the world
daily.

So far, we have said that we have
two groups, therefore two means,
two standard deviations. We are
interested in deciding whether the
difference between the two means
is reliable, i.e., that it is not a
chance event, that it is, in a sense,
real. We find the t, which is
actually a z, that is, it tells us
where on the curve this difference
falls.

Ok, you say. *So, we find the t
which is like z, then what?*

If our sample is large the t
distribution is identical to the
normal distribution. In the normal

distribution, we have seen that z of
1.96 is an important mark.
Between -1.96 and +1.96 95% of
the curve falls. A score (here a
difference) that falls within these
two marking points, has a
probability of 95% to occur by
chance in a known situation in
which there is no difference, that is
in a situation in which the two
samples were drawn from the
same population. That is what our
curve of no difference graphs.

If our sample is small? you ask.

While in the normal distribution
1.96 always marks the 95% of the
curve, in the t distribution it is so
only if the sample size is very
large. With smaller samples, 1.96
increases inversely proportional to
sample size. The smaller the
sample size, the greater the
increase in 1.96.

Remember, again, Gosset' s goal

STATISTICS FOR COLLEGE STUDENTS AND RESEARCHERS

was to make it difficult for
researchers to find significance
with small samples. He calculated
these new values of 1.96.

STATISTICS FOR COLLEGE STUDENTS AND RESEARCHERS

Drama
Mercy Mr. Gosset

Mr. Gosset, good morning. This is Samir calling from India. I ran an experiment with 20 subjects. How much should I increase 1.96?

Half asleep, Gosset takes out his notes and read the value to Samir.

The new value for z 1.96, the t, is 2.101.
Good night Mr. Samir.

Two hours later the phone rings again.

Good evening, Mr. Gosset. I am Michel Duzed, calling from Montreal Canada. Please give me the value of z for an experiment with 72 subjects.
Gosset looks at his notes and says:

It is 1.994
Goodnight.

STATISTICS FOR COLLEGE STUDENTS
AND RESEARCHERS

Going back to sleep is difficult for Mr.
Gosset. One hour later the phone
rings again, this time from Japan.

*Good day Mr. Gosset. Please give me
the new z for an experiment with 402
subjects.*

1.966, Gosset says, and he hangs up.
I got to do something about this, he
says, *aside from pulling the phone
from the plug. I got to do something…
I will never be able to sleep.*

He did. He published his notes
with the recalculated z of 1.96.
Have you seen this in any
statistics book? All of my students
say no, actually a lot of my
colleagues say no, too. I will
disclose the secret. It is the
famous t-table found at the end of
every statistics book, including the
one you are reading now (see
Appendix). Promise to keep our secret
between us.

STATISTICS FOR COLLEGE STUDENTS AND RESEARCHERS

Climax in the drama.

Samir of India wrote down the t value:
2.101

With hands trembling he picked up the sheet with the data analysis of his thesis to find the result of the t-test. He read it out aloud:

t=2.24
I made it! I made it!

he chants as he dances around in his room. Samir will get his Masters. The difference between the two means of his experiment is reliable.

He will report his finding as *significant.* In his thesis he will write:

This difference is significant (p<0.05).

STATISTICS FOR COLLEGE STUDENTS AND RESEARCHERS

What does this notation mean?

It means that the chance that his finding is not reliable, i.e., that it is a chance event, is less than 5 per cent.Scientists have agreed to accept findings as being reliable if the p value is less than 0.05.

Scientists have agreed to accept findings as being reliable, if the p value is less than 0.05.

Remember this!

STATISTICS FOR COLLEGE STUDENTS AND RESEARCHERS

Back in Canada Michel Duzed, holding the note with the t value that Mr. Gosset just gave her (it was 1.994, remember?), compares it with the result of the t-test value that she got by analyzing the data of her experiment, which was t=1.982.

Alas! The t she computed by using the t formula is smaller than the t Mr. Gosset gave her.

Her eyes open wide, her face get gloomy, and she collapses on an armchair. Michel will not get her Doctorate. Her finding is not significant. She will not write her dissertation. If she were to write it, she would report it as follows.

This finding is not significant (p>0.05). P greater than 0.05.

This means that her difference could have been a chance event more than 5 times in a hundred.

Michel quits graduate school, she marries

her sweetheart and moves out of Quebec
to a job as a business consultant.

What happened to the Japanese
guy?

His finding was significant too. But
he never got his Doctorate because
he refused to write up his thesis.
He joined the ABD club. Eventually
I hear he became a famous poet.
What does ABD mean? Figure it
out, or wait till you are about to
write up your doctoral thesis
yourself.

***Encore* the concepts.**

Before giving an example of the
t-test, we will launch a final attack
on the conceptual difficulties of the
t-test and inferential statistics in
general.

First let us refresh our memory.

STATISTICS FOR COLLEGE STUDENTS
AND RESEARCHERS

Between standard deviation or z -1.96 and +1.96, 95% of the curve lies. It follows that the remaining of the curve beyond -1.96 and +1.96 represents 5% or the curve.

Standard deviation 1.96
Percent of curve 95%
Standard deviation 2.56
Percent of curve 99%

The *curve of no difference*, as we said, has zero in the middle, that is the mean is zero.

What does this curve graph?
Remember the curve in the case of the woolen caps for the farmers of the State of Wisconsin?

That curve was a curve that we would be getting if we were allowed to collect many samples, figure out the mean of each, and graph these means. In effect this curve was empty.

But remember we knew
something about it. We knew the
estimate of the standard deviation
(*standard error of the mean*). We
calculated it from the standard
deviation of the one and only
sample mean we had.
In our present case, the t-curve is
a similar curve. It would be
graphing differences between two
means, if were we allowed to run
our experiment of two groups
many times, each time having two
means, calculating the mean of
each group and then calculating
the difference of the two means.

Because we have the standard
deviation of this curve, we can
consider our difference as a score
and engage in the ritual dance of
where my score falls. What point
on the standard deviation line
does this score (difference) lie.
We used the z formula to tell us

where on the curve our difference
lies. We said above that the
t-formula is actually a z formula, a
modified one, to take into account
the sample size. Let's look at them
again.

$$z = \frac{(X - \overline{X})}{s}$$

$$t = \frac{\overline{X_1} - \overline{X_2}}{\sqrt{\dfrac{s_1{}^2}{n_1}} + \sqrt{\dfrac{s_2{}^2}{n_2}}}$$

z equals score minus the mean divided by the standard deviation.

t equals score (mean 1 minus mean 2 gives us the difference which we consider to be a score) divided by the standard deviation (the standard deviation of both groups; remember that the square root of variance is the standard deviation).

You see then that the t is a z.

Why is the variance of each group divided by the number of subjects in the group?

Remember, Gosset's goal was to
make it difficult to researchers to
find significance if their sample
size was small.

**Understanding the logic of the
t-curve, the curve of no
difference.**

Drama
Me minus me equals 1

Professor Lilly Prydum, a statistician,
decided to run a simple experiment to test
a model for guessing if two means came
from one specific group, or they came
from two different groups.

Quite convoluted, you say.

She invited Memy Tallibum, Ph.D. in
Education, to be part of the experiment
and try to guess if the difference of two
means came from the same group, or not.

STATISTICS FOR COLLEGE STUDENTS AND RESEARCHERS

The subjects were 30 students from Trenton College. They were asked to take a test of 120 questions on Chinese geography, mythology, and culture. The scoring of the test was done by a computer, and the recording of the data was done in such a way that the subjects remained anonymous. The experiment lasted 35 days. Subjects were asked not to read about China during this time period. They were also asked not to chat amongst themselves and not to compare notes.

Day 1 of the experiment. Time 9:00 in the morning. The test is given. Time allotted 1 hour. 10:00 a.m. the testing period is over. Students are asked to take a 30 minute break. During that time the exam papers are graded, and the score is recorded next to each subject. Dr. Tallibum gets a copy of the results and studies them with care.

At 10:30 the students are called back in again, and are given the same test, the one they took 30 minutes earlier. At

11:30 the testing session is over. The subjects are thanked, and asked to be back the next day. "Please be back here at 9:00 in the morning sharp. And remember, no reading on China".

The students leave, their exam papers are graded, and the score of each student is recorded. Each subject now has two scores. The score from session 1 and the score from session 2. Dr. Tallibum gets a copy and scrutinizes it. As expected the difference between the first session and the second is very small, and for most students it is zero.

The next day all students are present, Dr. Tallibum is present, and the experiment proceeds as planned.

Session 1, the students are given the same test they took the previous day. Session
2, the students are given the same test. Scores are recorded and are handed to Dr. Tallibum who watches like a hawk. At the end of the second day Dr. Tallibum is not

surprised to see that, once again, the
difference between the first and the
second session is very small, close to zero.
Students are reminded that the
experiment will last 35 days, and asked to
"come back tomorrow ".

On day 16 of the experiment Dr. Tallibum
is surprised to see that the difference
between the first and the second session
is substantial. Students did not score as
well in the second session. The
explanation came in the evening as she
was watching the news. Pop star Mickey
Wiggletuchs had died. Students must have
heard about this during the break between
the two sessions and were emotionally
disturbed. That influenced their
performance in the second session.

On day 33 Dr. Tallibum was shocked to
see that the difference between session 1
and session 2 was so great. Scores in the
second session were so low! Again the
explanation came in the evening news.
The stock market had crashed. Apparently
the students heard of this disaster during

the break between the two sessions. Most likely parents called and told their children that there would be no money to pay the college fees.

Day 34, the day before the last day of the experiment, rolls smoothly. At the end of the second session, Dr. Tallibum is asked to leave the exam room.

Students are given the same instructions as usual. They are told to be present as usual, for the last day of the experiment.

Dr. Tallibum is left in the dark, she does not know what the students were told.

Day 35, the last day of the experiment.

Session 1. Students are taking the test as in the past and Dr. Tallibum is present, as in the past. During the break the exam papers are graded and scores handed to Dr. Tallibum.

STATISTICS FOR COLLEGE STUDENTS AND RESEARCHERS

At this point, there is a dramatic change in the procedure. Dr. Tallibum is asked to leave the exam room. She is led to the elevator and taken to the biology laboratories on the top floor, where there are no windows. She is asked not to leave this lab, not to make any phone calls, and wait there for an hour. To make sure, she is guarded by the graduate students of the biology lab.

At 11:30 the second session of the experiment is over. The students are told that the experiment came to an end, that there was no need for them to come back again, and were given a brief talk as to the purpose of the experiment.

The papers were graded, the scores were recorded and Professor Lilly Prydum, the experimenter, took the elevator to the Biology Lab and handed the results to Dr. Tallibum.

STATISTICS FOR COLLEGE STUDENTS
AND RESEARCHERS

Dr. Tallibum, she said. *In the second session we prevented you from seeing who were the subjects. As you realize we may have used the same subjects, the students from Trenton College, or we may have used another group. We could have used workers from the Physical Plant of the College, students from Trenton High, or senior citizens from the local senior citizens club. Your task is to guess whether the group that took the test during today's second session of the experiment were the Trenton College students that you watched for 35 days, or another, different group.*

Dr. Tallibum looked at the data sheet. It contained the difference between session 1 and session 2 for 35 days. The difference score of day 35 was the score in question.

Instinctively, her eyes ran up and down the list of differences. She was trying to find if the score of day 35 has occurred in the past 34 days. Not only that. If it has occurred, how often has it occurred. If she finds that it has occurred many times, she will conclude that the students in the second session of today were the same students, that is the Trenton College students.

If the difference score of today is not on the list, if it has never occurred in the last 34 days, then the wisest guess would be that in the second session of today it was not the Trenton College students that took the test.

It will be more difficult to guess if the difference of day 35 has occurred a few times, very few times. That's where Dr. Tallibum will resort to her knowledge of statistics. Guess what. She will draw Goddess Normal Curve and pray. Let's listen to her reasoning out loud:

Dr. Tallibum's soliloquy

The solution to my problem must be in the normal curve, as always. What do I have here. I have a difference between two means but I do not know if the two means came from the same group, or from two different groups. I want to guess wisely. I will start by placing 0 in the middle of the normal curve. This is the curve of no difference. I assume that this curve graphs differences between means that come from a known case, a case in which all means come from the same group, the same people. If the difference that I am not sure about is 0 or close to 0, I can safely conclude that this difference comes from the same group of people, i.e., that in both sessions of day 35 it was the Trenton College students that took the test. If the difference in question is large ...ay, there's the rub. Whether it safer to say same or not say, and suffer the slings and arrows of rough ridicule, or to shut up and by going against my promise to participate, my participation end. But behold, there is light. I can compute the standard deviation of this no-difference curve and reason. I can engage in the archetypal dance.

Behold Dr. Tallibum dancing around the

biology lab to the amazement of the bio graduate students.

I have a difference between the two means. I hold this difference up, wave it in the air, I baptize it score. Then I wear my glasses and stick my nose on the normal curve, running up and down the line with standard deviations on it, and mumble: where does this score fall? Where does this score fall?

I then use the z formula and find where exactly my score - oops, our difference - falls. If it falls within -1.96 and +1.96 then this score occurs frequently, 95% of the time, in this case of known no difference. If this score, difference, falls beyond 1.96 then it is a rare occurrence.

In this case the wisest guess is that it does not come from the same group, that is, in the second session it was not the Trenton students but another different group of people.

I hear a question. Speak up.

Can she find out what was this
new group, you say.
Yes, the Oracle of Delphi should
be able to tell you that.

Drama
The long jump

The prototypic experimenter is standing in the middle of the normal curve holding his score or difference in his hand. He is focusing on 1.96 and is about to jump beyond it. If he succeeds in jumping over 1.96, he gets a medallion (his degree perhaps); if he does not succeed, he lands on his behind, and gets a kick on the same.

Talking seriously now. All statistical tests are based on the same logic we developed above. So, I advise you to read my theatrical masterpieces carefully if you want to get the concepts, and be able to reason in statistics, and solve the problems with only 5 formulas.

STATISTICS FOR COLLEGE STUDENTS
AND RESEARCHERS

What are these 5 formulas?

The five formulas we need to know:

$$z = \frac{(X - \overline{X})}{s}$$

$$SEM = \frac{s}{\sqrt{n}}$$

$$s^2 = \frac{\Sigma(X - \overline{X})^2}{n}$$

$$t = \frac{\overline{X_1} - \overline{X_2}}{\sqrt{\frac{{s_1}^2}{n_1}} + \sqrt{\frac{{s_2}^2}{n_2}}}$$

$$F = \frac{MS_{between}}{MS_{within}}$$

STATISTICS FOR COLLEGE STUDENTS AND RESEARCHERS

An example of the t-test

A sports physiologist suspected that bouillon cubes may improve the performance of runners. She got this idea when she read a 1996 experiment of mine in the Journal of Physiology and Behavior. She randomly selected 12 U of I male undergraduates and randomly assigned them to either group 1 who were given a cup of soup with a bouillon cube, or group 2 who were given a cup of chamomile.

She subsequently asked the students to run a 100 meter course and recorded the time they took to reach the finish line.

Here is the layout of the experiment.

STATISTICS FOR COLLEGE STUDENTS AND RESEARCHERS

GROUP 1 BOUILLON	GROUP 2 NO BOUILLON
SUBJECT 1	SUBJECT 7
SUBJECT 2	SUBJECT 8
SUBJECT 3	SUBJECT 9
SUBJECT 4	SUBJECT 10
SUBJECT 5	SUBJECT 11
SUBJECT 6	SUBJECT 12

Note that a subject belongs to only one group, so the groups are independent. If subject 1 is John, and he belongs to the first group, he does not participate in the second group.

When the data were collected, she analyzed them by using the t-test. We say *she ran a t-test*.

The data and analysis are presented in the next table:

STATISTICS FOR COLLEGE STUDENTS AND RESEARCHERS

	Bouillon	**No Bouillon**
	34	48
	35	47
	39	45
	30	47
	39	46
	40	45
Mean	36.17	46.33
Variance	12.47	1.22
df	10	
t	6.14	
p	<0.05	

What do you mean by df? you
say. You look unhappy too.

In order to develop the concept of
degrees of freedom, df, we will run
a *tought experiment* (thought
experiment) as Einstein used to
say. The benefit will be that you
will not need to memorize any of
the many formulas for degrees of
freedom. Ever.

Drama
Mean Prophet

I take a sheet of paper from my printer
and cut it into four equal pieces. I take a
pencil and write the number 3 on the first
piece, I write number 4 on the second
piece, number 8 on the third piece, and
lastly number 5 on the fourth piece of
paper. I place all four pieces of paper in a
shoe box and put the cover on it so that
the pieces of paper cannot be seen. On
another sheet of paper I keep a record of
these four numbers. Then I add them up
3+4+8+5=20. Then I calculate the
average or mean.

20 divided by 4 equals 5. The mean is 5.
I destroy this piece of paper.

I take another sheet of paper and I write
on it the following:
Mean=5 n=4

I stick this paper on the shoe box for
anyone to see.

STATISTICS FOR COLLEGE STUDENTS AND RESEARCHERS

I ask Jerry, the English major who is sitting in the lounge, to come into the room. I explain to him that there are 4 pieces of paper in the box, each having a number on it. The mean of those numbers is 5. That is all he is told.

I begin by asking Jerry:
Jerry, close your eyes, stick your hand in the shoe box and pick one of the four pieces of paper.
Jerry does that. Before he draws his hand out of the box I ask him to guess the number he has picked.
Jerry giggles.

I am not a magician, he says.

Open your eyes and read out the number.

Eight, he says.

I lay the piece of paper with the number 8 down on the table so that it can be seen at glance at anytime.

STATISTICS FOR COLLEGE STUDENTS
AND RESEARCHERS

Now Jerry, stick your hand again in
the shoebox and pick another piece
of paper. Jerry does so. Before he
draws his hand out of the box, I
ask him to guess the number he
has picked.

Again, Jerry giggles and mumbles:
No way!

Open your eyes and read the
number out loud.

Five, he says.

I lay the piece of paper on the
table next the first one that Jerry
picked, the one that has the
number 8 on it. It can easily be
seen. There are two pieces of
papers on the table now with the
numbers, 8 and 5.

I repeat the procedure for the third time.

Jerry, can you guess what the number that
you drew?

STATISTICS FOR COLLEGE STUDENTS
AND RESEARCHERS

He smiles faintly and simply shrugs his shoulders.

Open your eyes and read the number out loud.

Four, he says.

Again, I lay the piece of paper with the number 4 on the table, next to the other two. There are three numbers on the table now: 8 and 5 and 4.

We are ready to repeat the procedure, I say. Close your eyes and stick …

Before I can finish my sentence, Jerry says:

Number 3.

Great! Jerry knows simple arithmetic. He added up the numbers he had already drawn.

8+5+4=17. There is only one number which, if added to 17, will give 20. That is the number 3.

There is only one number that
divided by 4 will give us a mean of
5. That number is 20.

What am I to get out of this story?
you say.

Without knowing the mean and the
n (how many numbers) you could
not guess any of the numbers.
They were free to vary. Several
arrays of four numbers could give
us a sum of 20. For example
11+1+2+6=20, or 5+ 6+8+1=20.
Because I calculated the mean
and showed it to you, and I also
told you how many numbers there
are in the box, one of the numbers
is not free to vary.

In statistical language we say: We
lose one *degree of freedom* every
time we calculate a mean.

We lose one degree of freedom for every mean that we calculate.

Remember this.

The degrees of freedom in this case is 3, that is
4-1=3.

Formally we write it as follows:
df=3.

In another situation that we have two groups of 10 subjects each, 20 total, and we calculate two means the degrees of freedom are 18. That is, we subtract 1 for each mean we calculate. This is simple to remember. I am confident that you understand this concept at the gut level, not just repeating my words like a parrot.

As I promised you, we will push aside almost all the formulas that

otherwise you would have to
memorize.

It is logical, isn't it. If you know the
concept and you know what you
are doing, you do not need a
formula to tell you what to do step
by step.

Back to our discussion of the
t-test.

Definition: *t obtained.*

That is the result of solving for t. In
other words when you run a t-test
you find a t value. A third way of
saying this is: the result of
analyzing your data using the t
formula.

Definition: *t required.*

The required t is the value
contained in the t-table which is
found in the end of every statistics
book, including the one you are

STATISTICS FOR COLLEGE STUDENTS AND RESEARCHERS

reading now (see Appendix).

Remember, the t-table lists the modified 1.96 that Gosset published. It lists the recalculated values for 1.96 depending on degrees of freedom.

To find the required t, you first calculate the degrees of freedom. You are an expert in calculating degrees of freedom (df). No formulas needed, not for us who learn statistics by acting in soap operas.

In the present example of the t-test (page 114) we have two groups of 6 subjects each, total of 12 subjects. Since in computing the t we need to first compute the mean of each group, two means, we lose 2 degrees of freedom. How many scores go into the calculation of the t? All of the scores. That is,12 scores, minus 2 equals 10. Therefore, df=10.

STATISTICS FOR COLLEGE STUDENTS AND RESEARCHERS

Now we go to the t table in Appendix and run our finger down the left column which is labeled df. We stop at 10. Then we draw out finger horizontally until we reach the column that is labeled 5% or 0.05. We copy the value we find at the tip of our finger. This is the required t.

We compare this with the obtained t, i.e., the one that we calculated. If the obtained t is larger than the required t, we have significance. We say that our finding (the difference between the two means) is reliable or significant. This means that we trust that, if we run the same experiment again, we will find a difference again.

We formally write this as follows:

The difference between the means of the two groups is significant ($p<0.5$).

STATISTICS FOR COLLEGE STUDENTS AND RESEARCHERS

By that we mean that the finding we are reporting is reliable, but there is still a chance that it may not be "real". That chance is less than five per cent. Scientists around the world have agreed to accept findings for which the probability of being chance events and not "real" is less than five percent. You understand correctly, there is no absolute certainty in experimental natural science. Findings are taken to be "true" on a probability basis. You see that boring, compulsive statistics borders on philosophy if approached from the correct angle.

One last remark. It is really unwarranted to speak of truth in dealing with phenomena in the empirical, material world. We can only speak of truth in the formal, logical and mathematical sciences.

STATISTICS FOR COLLEGE STUDENTS AND RESEARCHERS

Two plus three equals five. This
is true. Two plus three is
six, is false. It makes no sense to
say that the statement: "Valium at
doses of 2, 5, 10, and 20 mg
reduces anxiety" is true. It is
simply reliable and there is a
probability attached to it, no matter
how small, that it may not be so.

STATISTICS FOR COLLEGE STUDENTS AND RESEARCHERS

Lecture 6

Analysis of variance

One-way ANOVA

Analysis of variance is used by scientists in order to analyze data from experiments of literally unlimited experimental designs. It is most popular and dominant statistical test in the biological and social sciences. The complexity of these designs ranges from very simple to frighteningly convoluted. The formulas are so many that no statistical book contains all of them.

As I promised you, we will navigate through this ocean with no formulas. We do not need them. If we understand what we are doing, if we get the concepts involved, we do not need formulas. Do you need a map in order to work around your kitchen?

Hurray, here we launch the big ocean liner, ANOVA!

What is ANOVA, what do we do in

Analysis of Variance?

We analyze variance.

That is tautologous, you say.
Ok, we partition the variance. That
is pretty much what we do.

Variance I know well, you say.

Analysis of Variance you know
pretty well, I say.

Yes. Variance we know so well.

$$s^2 = \frac{\sum (X - \bar{X})^2}{n - 1}$$

Remember? The sum of squared
deviations of each score from the
mean, and all of this divided by n,
the number of scores that went
into the calculation, i.e., here, the

number of all scores.

Why do you say "here", you ask.

Good observation. n does not always represent the number of scores in an experiment. It is the number of observations, that is a safer way to say this. More of that soon. I was saying that what we do in ANOVA is analyze the variance in our data, more specifically, we *partition* the variance.

What is the result of this analysis? Is it a t?

Something like a t. A modified t, I would say.

You said earlier that it is a modified z.

t is a modified z
F is a modified t?

You are very observant. Yes. As I
told you earlier, statistics is like a
pyramid. Discoveries are based
on earlier discoveries.
There is continuity. If you brush
aside the many formulas and
concentrate on concepts, you get
a marvelous view of the edifice of
statistics. Then you are in
command. You can take decisions,
be in a position to critically view
experiments, defend yourself
against criticism that is thrown at
you, and ultimately add this
knowledge to your personal
philosophy.

Drama
Clip his tail

Fisher was determined to clip Gosset 's tail
a bit.

That Gosset, *he thinks he is smart. He
rides high in the world with his stupid
t-distribution. Big deal! All he did was to*

STATISTICS FOR COLLEGE STUDENTS AND RESEARCHERS

add one puny column on the left of the normal distribution. The df column. Oh, yes, ok, ok...He did recalculate the z, big deal.

Fisher had been scratching his head for months, engaging in obsessive dialogues with Gosset, downgrading his achievement but deep down he knew he was jealous.

I got to come up with something myself. What if I add another column to the normal distribution. Another column of what? Not df again? If not df, what then. I got to be more original. How about another line on top of the t table.
He did. The df Between.
Good Knighthood, Sir Fisher.

The result, the endpoint of
ANOVA, is F. This is in honoring
Fisher who developed ANOVA.
We calculate the F by the so
called F ratio which is:

$$F = \frac{MS_{between}}{MS_{within}}$$

We read this as follows:

F equals mean square between,
divided by mean square within.

Remember that mean square is
another way of saying variance.
So, you should not be worried with
the F ratio.

What about between and within?
you say.

That is easy. In computing the
variance between we calculate a

variance. We line up the means of
the various groups in our
experiment, we treat them like
scores, and figure out the
variance.

You are kidding, you say. *I have
seen terrifying formulas for even
the simplest ANOVA.*

You are correct.

Now the second part of your
question. Mean square within.
Easy again. You already know it.
We compute the variance of the
first group, and write it down, then
we compute the variance of the
second group and write it down,
then we do the same for all the
groups in our experiment. The
number of groups can vary from 2
to as many as you wish. In the end
we simply add these variances.
That gives the variance within.

Amazing! you say. *No new*

formulas for ANOVA!

You can use ANOVA right away. All you needed was to get the concepts of variance between and variance within.

What about partitioning the variance? you say.

Variance between and variance within, if added together, give us the Total variance.

Total variance can be computed if you calculate the variance of all the scores of all your groups, disregarding what group a score came from. Again, all you need is the familiar variance formula.

That is unbelievable, you say. *I am confused. Every statistics book gives ANOVA summary tables.*

Yes indeed. That is the convention, but it is not necessary

in order to compute the F ratio. In practically every case in which step by step instructions are given (without first developing the concepts) things acquire an aura of awesome complexity and difficulty, and, I am afraid, fake importance.

STATISTICS FOR COLLEGE STUDENTS AND RESEARCHERS

Because you and I cannot go against the whole world, let's take a quick look at the typical presentation of ANOVA. Up until the sixties, journals were including ANOVA summary tables in the publications. As I said, this gives a publication the semblance of quantitative science, but, alas, at times only a semblance.

ANOVA SUMMARY TABLE
One-way ANOVA

Source	SS	df	MS	F	p
Between					
Within					
Total					

We know every term on this table. *Within* is also called the *error* term. The error term is the term which goes in the denominator of the F ratio. In more complex designs, the error term may be other than the within term.

STATISTICS FOR COLLEGE STUDENTS AND RESEARCHERS

Review the five formulas that are needed for virtually all parametric statistics. Do not simply memorize them, look into them conceptually.

$$z = \frac{(X - \bar{X})}{s}$$

$$SEM = \frac{s}{\sqrt{n}}$$

$$s^2 = \frac{\sum (X - \bar{X})^2}{n - 1}$$

$$t = \frac{\bar{X_1} - \bar{X_2}}{\sqrt{\frac{s_1^2}{n_1}} + \sqrt{\frac{s_2^2}{n_2}}}$$

$$F = \frac{MS_{between}}{MS_{within}}$$

An example of ANOVA

A biologist wanted to see if quantity of vitamin C in diet may reduce body weight. He randomly selected 15 male rats and randomly assigned them to the following three groups. Group1 10 mg, Group2 20 mg, and Group3 30 mg. He added this vitamin in the food of the rats daily for 30 days. On the 30th day he weighed the rats.

STATISTICS FOR COLLEGE STUDENTS AND RESEARCHERS

Here are the data and the ANOVA table.

GROUP 1 10 mg	GROUP 2 20 mg	GROUP 3 30 mg
200	204	214
203	210	220
199	214	225
190	219	220
204	211	229
Mean 1 = 199.20	Mean 2 = 211.60	Mean 3 = 221.6
s = 5.54	s = 5.50	s = 5.68

STATISTICS FOR COLLEGE STUDENTS AND RESEARCHERS

ANOVA SUMMARY TABLE
One-way ANOVA

Source	SS	df	MS	F	P
Between	1259	2	629.6	20.24	<0.0001
Within	373.2	12	31.10		
Total	1632	14			

The analysis showed that we have a significant effect. The differences between the means are significant, i.e., reliable. The p value is less than 1 in 10000. This means that the probability that the difference we report is a chance event (and not the result of our treatment of giving rats vitamin C) is less than 1 in 10000.

How did you compute the degrees of freedom, df, you ask.

STATISTICS FOR COLLEGE STUDENTS AND RESEARCHERS

You know this if you know the concepts of Between, Within, and Total.

We said, in order to compute the variance between, we line up the means of all the groups and treat them as scores, and calculate the variance. How many means we have here? We have three means. We really consider them as scores here. In order to calculate the variance of three numbers, we must first calculate the mean. By calculating the mean, we lose 1 degree of freedom for every mean, remember? So, our df for the between term is 3-1=2.

We calculate variance within as we said above. We calculate the mean of the first group and then the variance of this group. Then we do the same for the second group, and then the third group. We add these 3 variances and this gives us the variance within. Since

STATISTICS FOR COLLEGE STUDENTS
AND RESEARCHERS

we compute 3 means in the
process of calculating the
variances, we lose 3 degrees of
freedom. How many scores went
into the calculations of variance
within? All the sores, that is 15.
Our degrees of freedom then are
df=15-3=12.

Easy, no formulas needed,
because we understand the
concept of df and also variance
within.

Lastly, we compute the df of Total
as follows:

In order to compute the Total
variance, we said, we take all of
the scores of all the groups
disregarding what group each
score comes from. In order to
calculate this variance we must
first calculate the mean, therefore
we lose 1 degree of freedom. How
many scores went into the
calculation of the Total variance?

All of the scores, here 15. Our
degrees of freedom for Total then
is 15-1=14.

Note that adding up the df for
Between and Within we find the df
for Total.

That is what we meant by
partitioning. We said we partition
variance.

Here we partition the Total
 variance into variance
between and variance within.
Indeed, verify that SS between
plus SS within equals SS Total.
That is,
$1259 + 373.2 = 1632.2$
How did we get the p value? you
ask.

I will be very practical here. As
was the case with the t-distribution,
here too, there is a table with the F
values (see Appendix).

These are in a way the recalculated 1.96, that is the point on the curve beyond which 5% of the curve lies.

In the case of the t curve we entered the table with the degrees of freedom and found the required t at the 5% level. In the present case, we enter the F table with the degrees of freedom for Between (in the present experiment df=2) and the degrees of freedom for Within (in the present experiment df=12). We locate the F on the table. This is the required F.

Then we compare the obtained F (the one we calculated, look at he summary table) to the required F. As in the case of the t-test, if our obtained F is greater than the required F, we have significance. We then say $p < 0.05$.

I understand how we calculate df without formulas, however I do not see why we need it.

I see why you are confused. As I
said this is what happens every
time we try to teach in a
mechanistic, compulsive, step by
step way. The general practice of
working with formulas blindly, and
using the ANOVA summary table,
often prevents the student from
seeing what is going on.
As I said at the beginning, the
ANOVA summary table is not
needed. What you need to do is
simply calculate the variance, and
compare the variances, that is the
F ratio. df is simply the n in the
variance formula.

df is simply the n in the variance
formula

I understand variance Between,

variance Within, and df.
However, I do not see why the F
ratio can detect significance, you
say.

A very important question, if
indeed, we are sincere when we
say we want to understand the
concepts and the logic of statistics.

STATISTICS FOR COLLEGE STUDENTS AND RESEARCHERS

Drama
Master of the waves

It is a beautiful, cool, calm day in Puerto Rico. You are sitting in a San Juan small café, nested on the rocks overlooking the magnificent Atlantic ocean. You are happy, sipping your coffee, Bacardi on the side, and slowly nibbling on a sinfully sweet piece of PR cake. It is quiet, the only thing you hear is the rhythmic sound of waves gently breaking on the foundations of the cafe. Suddenly you hear voices; it sounds like people are arguing. Soon their voices become loud enough, you can clearly hear what they are saying.

You don't believe me? Look again. See? I caused that wave.

There is much laughter.

Buddy, you are nuts, that's what I say. The only waves you cause is in your brain. You go and see a shrink!

The argument grows in intensity and the guy with the claims to supernatural powers, keeps throwing small stones into the sea. You decide to join the noisy group and get the argument straight.

Guys, I have the answer to your argument. I will show you who is right. For now, let the sea rest and calm down, just in case this guy has disturbed it. Come sit and have a cup of coffee.

Ten minutes later, you take the lot to the edge of the rocks.

First, we will measure the heights of the next 40 waves and record these data, you say.

When forty waves have been recorded, you turn to the guy with the supernatural claims and say:

Ok, this is your show now.

The guy, his confidence somewhat deflated,

picks up a stone and hurls it into the sea. All
eyes are fixed on the base of the rock,
waiting for the next wave. The wave comes
and is recorded.

The moment of truth, you say.

The height of the wave is read out loud. It is
not taller than any of the 40 waves
previously recorded. The miracle worker
receives a truckload of cosmetic epithets and
soon the café slips back into the beatific
serenity. Sleep hovers over your eyelids.
You dream of conquistadors and fierce
Carib Indians, of rituals and dances that
humans created in an attempt to understand
their world.

*Cute story, but I still do not
understand why the F ratio can
indeed measure that we have
significance,* you say.

The forty waves provided us with
what I call the "endogenous"
variance, baseline, the variation in
the heights of the waves that is

present when no obvious cause can be seen. The wave after the action of the ambitious miracle worker was the presumed effect of his manipulation (in statistics we call this *treatment)*. Comparing the baseline with the claimed effect of his manipulation can give us support, or lack thereof, for a connection between what he did and the result we observed.

If the result which he claims that he caused by his manipulation is bigger than the natural, (endogenous or spontaneous variance), then we may say that he caused the effect by his manipulation.

A brief parenthesis at this point to make sure we understand what we mean by saying ratio. Alas, mechanistic methods of teaching arithmetic without development of concepts, often prevent the pupil from understanding that in division, what we do is compare two numbers: the numerator to the denominator. If you have 20 dollars, and I have 5 dollars, in dividing 20 by 5, I compare 20 to 5. You have 4 times more money than I have.

Our treatment causes variance between to increase? you say.

Yes, let's see it in an example.

A pharmacologist is testing a new drug (tentatively named Coolx) that is suspected to lower body temperature. He randomly selects 10 male college students and randomly assigns them to two groups. Group 1 receives Coolx, Group 2 receives a placebo (an inert substance that has no effect on physiology).

Here is the layout of the experiment.

Group 1 Coolx	Group 2 Placebo
Subject 1	Subject 6

STATISTICS FOR COLLEGE STUDENTS AND RESEARCHERS

Subject 2	Subject 7
Subject 3	Subject 9
Subject 4	Subject 9
Subject 5	Subject 10

Before the experiment proper, the pharmacologist records the temperature of the subjects, in order to have the baseline temperature, the temperature that is present without any manipulation on the part of the experimenter.

Here is the baseline temperature (Celsius)

STATISTICS FOR COLLEGE STUDENTS
AND RESEARCHERS

Group 1 - Coolx		Group 2 - placebo	
Subject 1	36.9	Subject 6	37.0
Subject 2	37.0	Subject 7	36.6
Subject 3	36.7	Subject 8	36.3
Subject 4	36.4	Subject 9	36.8
Subject 5	36.7	Subject 10	36.9
Mean 1 = 36.740		Mean 2 = 36.720	
Variance 1 = 0.053		Variance 2 = 0.077	

We will now calculate variance between.

Remember, in order to calculate variance between we line up the means and treat them as scores. We then proceed and calculate the variance of these scores.

STATISTICS FOR COLLEGE STUDENTS AND RESEARCHERS

Here we have two means
36.740   36.720
The variance of these two scores
is 0.053. This is variance between.

The next table shows temperature
after the administration of drug
Coolx to Group 1

Group 1 - Coolx		Group 2 - placebo	
Subject 1	36.9	Subject 6	37.0
Subject 2	37.0	Subject 7	36.6
Subject 3	36.7	Subject 8	36.3
Subject 4	36.4	Subject 9	36.8
Subject 5	36.7	Subject 10	36.9
Mean 1 = 36.740		Mean 2 = 36.720	
Variance 1 = 0.053		Variance 2 = 0.077	

Note that the mean in Group 1
decreased. It was 36.740 before

giving the drug, it is 35.94 now.
Also note that the variance of this
group did not change.

Now the big moment has arrived.
Has the variance between
changed? If yes, we will be
convinced that variance between
is sensitive to our manipulation,
i.e., that it senses the effect of the
drug.

As usual, in order to calculate
variance between, we line up the
means and treat them as scores.
We then calculate the variance of
these scores.

The means here are:

35.94 36.720

The variance is 0.3042.
This is variance between.

Let's compare this to variance
between before our manipulation

of giving the drug:

We saw above that variance was 0.053 .

Voila! After giving the drug, that is after our treatment, variance between changed. Variance within did not change.

Conclusion: The F ratio is sensitive to our treatment. It does so, because variance Between changes because of our manipulation, while variance Within does not change.

Why? you say.

Remember that variance measures the distance of scores from the mean. The mean can increase or decrease but the distance of scores from the mean does not change. The scores move up or down *with* the mean.

STATISTICS FOR COLLEGE STUDENTS
AND RESEARCHERS

Lecture 7

Analysis of Variance

Factorial Designs

Two-Way ANOVA

The ANOVA that we discussed so
far is called 'One-way ANOVA' or
'Single-factor ANOVA'.

Now we will consider two-way
ANOVA or two-factor ANOVA.

The concepts we developed so far
also apply to two-way ANOVA.

*What do you mean by one-way,
single-factor, two-way, or
two-factor?* you say.

STATISTICS FOR COLLEGE STUDENTS
AND RESEARCHERS

Drama
Beam storm

Rutgers College. May 9, 1999, 9:00 in the morning. Two sections of Statistics 101 are in class: two adjacent classrooms, C120 and C121. USS Spaceship Enterprise flew over the two classrooms and locked on the bio readings of the students. Then, classroom C120 was bombarded with a X-Z-LOBX beam for 10 milliseconds. The security cameras recorded an almost imperceptible tilt of the head to the left, while the professor of Statistics, without being aware, wrote the same complex formula for MS 5 times. Two nanoseconds after classroom C120 was bathed in the benevolent X-Z-LOBX beam, classroom C121 was bombarded by the same X-Z-LOBX beam for 100 milliseconds. All students raised the index finger of their right hand and stuck it in their left nostril. The professor started reciting the t-table but stopped short in a deluge of laughter from the students.

The duration of the students' responses was recorded by the spaceship and instantly transmitted to Houston where a robot was waiting to manually enter the data on the layout of the experiment. The layout of the experiment was made public, the data not. Discussion of data was forbidden by a unanimous decision of the Congress.

The layout of the USS Enterprise experiment

10 ms	100 ms
Classroom C120 Student 1 Student 2 etc	**Classroom C121** Student 50 Student 51 etc

This experiment is a one-way ANOVA design.

Why? Because each student was bombarded with one beam.
We also say that this design is a single-factor ANOVA.

Why?

Because each student was
bombarded with a single beam.
Another way of saying this is, that
each score in this experiment is
the result of one beam, one factor,
or one treatment. You may also
 come across the term
one-way classification.

What we do to the subjects is
called:
independents variable
or *treatment*

Now it will be easy for us to
understand two-way ANOVA.

**An example of a two-way
ANOVA**

A psychiatrist wanted to see
whether a combination of wine
and vitamin C may have an effect
on depression.

He randomly selected 10 male
patients, and also 10 female
patients, and randomly assigned
them in two groups: wine group, or
vitamin C group.
.

The layout of this experiment is
presented in the next table:

STATISTICS FOR COLLEGE STUDENTS
AND RESEARCHERS

	wine	vitamin C
male	subject 1 subject 2 subject 3 subject 4 subject 5	subject 6 subject 7 subject 8 subject 9 subject 10
female	subject 11 subject 12 subject 13 subject 14 subject 15	subject 16 subject 17 subject 18 subject 19 subject 20

Look at subject 1. This subject is
influenced by two variables. Male
gender, and also wine. The score
of depression that he will give, will
be the result of these two factors.
For this reason, we call this type of
experiment a two-factor
experiment. The same, of course,
holds for all subjects. They are, in
a way, under crossfire. Two
factors hit them.

The layout above can also be
given in a more abstract form.

STATISTICS FOR COLLEGE STUDENTS AND RESEARCHERS

Variable A is gender, variable B is nutrition. Each variable has two levels, a1 a2 and b1 b2

	b1	b2
a1	subject 1 subject 2 subject 3 subject 4 subject 5	subject 6 subject 7 subject 8 subject 9 subject 10
a2	subject 11 subject 12 subject 13 subject 14 subject 15	subject 16 subject 17 subject 18 subject 19 subject 20

We say: We have two variables, A and B. A is gender, B is nutrition. Each of these two variables has two levels. a1, a2, and b1, b2. Because in this experiment we use 2 variables with 2 levels each, we call this experiment *2 x 2 factorial*. We read this as follows:

two by two factorial.

STATISTICS FOR COLLEGE STUDENTS AND RESEARCHERS

The ANOVA summary table for two-factor experiments is the following:

ANOVA SUMMARY TABLE
Two-Way, 2x2 Factorial

Source	SS	df	MS	F	p
Between A					
Between B					
A x B *					
Within					
Total					

* Also called interaction

Things are getting complicated, I hear you say.

I say: You already know everything in this new ANOVA.

Our approach of understanding
the concepts and not memorizing
formulas has paid out.

*Why do we have two Between
terms, A and B?* you say.

Because here we have two
variables: gender, and nutrition,
i.e., A and B. We want to know if
gender (being male or female) has
an effect, and also if nutrition (wine
or vitamin C) has an effect.
Remember, the Between term is
the term that senses the effects of
our treatments.

The Within term we also know. It is
the variance of each group
separately. The sum of these
variances.

The Total term we also know. It is
simply the variance of all scores
without regard to what group they
came from.

The interaction term is a Between
term for cells taken diagonally:
mean for a1b1+a2b2 and mean
a1b2+a2b1. Look at the layout to
visualize this.

	b1	b2
a1	subject 1 subject 2 subject 3 subject 4 subject 5	subject 6 subject 7 subject 8 subject 9 subject 10
a2	subject 11 subject 12 subject 13 subject 14 subject 15	subject 16 subject 17 subject 18 subject 19 subject 20

What is new here is the concept of
the interaction term. We need to
develop this concept, so we get a
gut feeling for it.

STATISTICS FOR COLLEGE STUDENTS AND RESEARCHERS

When you give two treatments to subjects, one of the things you want to see is whether the two variables interact with each other.

To begin developing the concept of interaction, let us consider a simple experiment:

We give 5 mg of an anti-anxiety drug, such as diazepam, and find that this results in an increase in the time patients sleep. This increase is 2 hours.

Using different subjects, we find that 200 ml of wine increase sleep time by 1 hour.

Now if we give both 5 mg of valium and 200 ml of wine, is it sure that we will get 3 hours increase in sleep time? Perhaps yes, perhaps no. We know that drugs may interact and produce dramatic results, if given together. You may have heard of cases in

which diazepam taken together
with alcohol caused coma, and
even death, because of
potentiation.

Students find the concept of
interaction difficult. For this reason
I will give an example later.

For the purposes of calculation of
this term in the ANOVA, there is no
problem. The df, as you would
expect, is the df of A x the df for B.

The SS you can calculate by
subtraction. SS total-(SS Between
A+SS Between B+SS within).

Alternatively, you can compute the
SS for AxB the same way you
calculated the between term, but
here calculate two means
diagonally, i.e.
mean for
a1b1+a2b2
and mean for
a2b1+a1b2.

Then we proceed with
the calculation of the variance of
these means.

The type of ANOVA design we are
discussing here is called *factorial*,
because in designing the
experiment we produce all
possible combinations.

In the above example we have:

Male - Wine, Male Vitamin C
Female - Wine, Female Vitamin C

Read this several times, it sounds
like a nursery rhyme. There is a
symmetry in it.

**Visualizing the layout of
factorial designs**

You will often come across
experiments that use these
designs, and if you go to graduate
school there is good chance you
will use them in your research.

We need to be able to visualize
the designs in order to understand
and evaluate them. A key
part of the task of a scientist is to
be able to critically evaluate the
research of others. Regrettably,
even reputable journals publish
research that is not sound.

STATISTICS FOR COLLEGE STUDENTS AND RESEARCHERS

We have considered so far a 2x2
design. How do we visualize this?
We see two characters (forget that
it is the number 2 here) separated
by the symbol x which stands for
times.

We have two things, two
variables, we therefore write down
A also B.

A   B

Now we look again at 2x2 and this
time pay attention to what number
we have. Here we have 2.
We therefore write
A
a1 a2

Then we look at the number after
the x. It is also 2 (mind you it does
not have to always be 2, it can be,
4, 10 any number).

We therefore write
B

b1 b2

To sum up:
a1b1 a1b2
a2b1 a2b2

Read this several times, it sounds
like a nursery rhyme. There is a
symmetry in it.

This is how we visualize a 2x2
factorial:

a1b1   a1b2
a2b1   a2b2

Now let us consider this: 2x3

How do we visualize this? We
see two characters (forget that it is
the numbers 2 and 3 here)
separated by the symbol x which
stands for *times*. We have two
things, two variables, we therefore
write down A and also B.

A   B

Now we look again at 2x3 and this
time pay attention to what
numbers we have. Before x we
have 2. We therefore write:
A
a1 a2

Then we look at the number after
the x. It is 3 (mind you, it does not
have to always be 3, it can be 4,
10, any number).

We therefore write:
B
b1 b2 b3

This is how we visualize a 2x3
factorial:
a1b1   a1b2 a1b3
a2b1   a2b2 a2b3

Now let us consider this: 2x3x5

How do we visualize this? We see
three characters (forget that it is
the numbers 2 and 3 and 5 here)
separated by the symbol x which
stands for *times*. We have three
things, three variables, we
therefore write down A, B,
also C.

A   B   C

Now we look again at 2x3x5 and
this time pay attention to what
numbers we have. Before x we
have 2.
We therefore write
A
a1 a2

Then we look at the number after
the x. It is 3 (mind you, it does not
have to always be 3, it can be, 4,
10, any number).
We therefore write

B

b1 b2 b3

Then we look at the third
number after the x. It is 5 (mind
you it does not have to always be
5, it can be, 6, 28, any number).
We therefore write

C

c1 c2 c3 c4 c5

**Examples of factorial
experiments
Example 1 of a 2x2 factorial.**

A pharmacology graduate student
working on his thesis wanted to
find whether a new chemical,
srt-X, which has been shown to
block serotonin, may be beneficial
to schizophrenic patients. He was
also interested to see if
electroshock has an effect on
these patients when combined
with srt-X.

He randomly selected 20
schizophrenic patients, and
randomly assigned them to 4
groups:

electroshock - srt-X,
electroshock-no srt-X
no electroshock - srt-X,
no electroshock-no srt-X

STATISTICS FOR COLLEGE STUDENTS AND RESEARCHERS

The layout of this experiment is:

	srt-X	no srt-X
electroshock	subject 1 subject 2 subject 3 subject 4 subject 5	subject 6 subject 7 subject 8 subject 9 subject 10
no electroshock	subject 11 subject 12 subject 13 subject 14 subject 15	subject 16 subject 17 subject 18 subject 19 subject 20

The layout in abstract form is:

	b1	b2
a1	subject 1 subject 2 subject 3 subject 4 subject 5	subject 6 subject 7 subject 8 subject 9 subject 10
a2	subject 11 subject 12 subject 13 subject 14 subject 15	subject 16 subject 17 subject 18 subject 19 subject 20

Variable A has two levels, a1 and a2, and variable B has two levels, b1 and b2.

The next table shows the data he recorded in running the experiment. The numbers represent scores on a psychiatric test measuring intensity of schizophrenic behavior. The higher the number the worse the condition of the patient.

STATISTICS FOR COLLEGE STUDENTS
AND RESEARCHERS

THE SEROTONIN BLOCKER
PLUS SHOCK EXPERIMENT

	b1	b2
a1	subject1 11 subject2 11 subject3 13 subject4 12 subject5 10 mean = 11.4 variance = 1.3	subject6 17 subject7 18 subject8 17 subject9 16 subject10 17 mean = 17 variance = 0.5
a2	subject11 15 subject12 14 subject13 14 subject14 16 subject15 15 mean = 14.8 variance = 0.7	subject16 20 subject17 19 subject18 18 subject19 20 subject20 18 mean = 16.9 variance = 1

STATISTICS FOR COLLEGE STUDENTS AND RESEARCHERS

ANOVA SUMMARY TABLE OF THE SEROTONIN BLOCKER PLUS SHOCK EXPERIMENT

Source	SS	df	MS	F	p
Between A	36.45	1	36.45	41.66	<.0001
Between B	120.05	1	120.05	137.2	<.0001
A x B *	2.45	1	2.45	2.8	>.05
Within	14	16	0.88		
Total	172.95	19			

* Interaction

I will first discuss the table in terms of the calculations we did.

First and most important, the degrees of freedom.
If you tell me the degrees of freedom in any ANOVA experiment, but without the use of formulas (I do also mean resorting to memory for the recollection of

formulas - ban formulas!), I know
you know what you are talking
about. Calculation of the F is easy,
high school arithmetic.

If you tell me the degrees of
freedom, I know you know how to analyze
that data.

Why df for Between A is 1?

Because in order to calculate
variance Between we line up the
means, consider them scores, and
calculate the variance using the
one and only formula for variance
(all the other formulas for variance
that you may see around are
derived from this formula.
Statisticians get their kicks by
producing equivalent formulas, of
considerable complexity and
ornamental value!). Now you and I
know that in order to calculate

variance, we must first calculate
the mean. Every time we calculate
the mean, we lose 1 degree of
freedom. Because, in the present
example we have 2 scores (never
mind that they are means), we are
left with 1 df. That is 2-1=1.

*I do not understand why you say
we have 2 means for A,* you ask.

Good question. A has two levels
here, a1 and a2. That is shock and
no shock. You see, when we deal
with variable A, we ignore variable
B. In other words we reduce this
part of the analysis to a one-way,
single-factor ANOVA.

Why df for Between B is 1? you
say.

For the same reasons as in the
previous paragraph, B has two
levels, b1 and b2, drug and no
drug. There are two means
(scores). In order to calculate the

variance of these two scores, we
must first compute the mean. We
therefore lose 1 df. So the df for B
is 2-1=1.

Why df for AxB interaction is 1?

This is easy. Since df for A is 1, and
df for B is also 1, the df for AxB is
1x1=1.
Why is the df for within 16?

This is simple, too. We said variance
within is variance for the first
group plus variance for the second
group, plus variance for the third
groups and so on. We have four
groups here. In order to calculate
the variance of each group we
must first calculate a mean. The
consequence of this is that we
lose 1 df for every mean we
calculate. How many scores go
into the calculation of variance for
group 1? Five scores. Therefore
df for the first group is 5-1=4. We
calculate the variance of the

STATISTICS FOR COLLEGE STUDENTS AND RESEARCHERS

remaining 3 groups in a similar way. Since we have 4 groups here, the df for Within is 4x4=16.

Note: Checksum. The sum of df for A, B, AxB, Within, equals df Total

SS for A, B, AxB, and Within equals SS Total.

Remember, we said that in ANOVA we partition variance.

**Discussion of the experiment
with the schizophrenic patients.**

Look at the ANOVA Table again:

ANOVA SUMMARY TABLE OF
THE SEROTONIN BLOCKER
PLUS SHOCK EXPERIMENT

Source	SS	df	MS	F	p
Between A	36.45	1	36.45	41.66	<.0001
Between B	120.05	1	120.05	137.2	<.0001
A x B *	2.45	1	2.45	2.8	>.05
Within	14	16	0.88		
Total	172.95	19			

* Interaction

The p value (the probability that
the difference or effect we are
reporting may not be reliable or
significant) for A is less than 1 in
ten thousand (p<.0001|).

STATISTICS FOR COLLEGE STUDENTS
AND RESEARCHERS

Variable A is electroshock in this experiment. This means that the two conditions, electroshock and no electroshock (condition 1: electroshock-drug, electroshock-no drug; condition 2: no-electroshock-drug, no- electroshock-no drug) produced a result, a significant difference.

In other words those patients who received electroshock ended up different from those patients that did not receive electroshock.

The p value (the probability that the difference or effect we are reporting may not be reliable or significant) for B is less than 1 in ten thousand ($p<.0001|$).

Variable B is drug in this experiment. This means that the two conditions, drug and no drug (condition 1: drug-electroshock, drug-no electroshock, condition 2: no drug-electroshock, no drug-no electroshock) produced a result, a significant difference. In other words, those patients who received the drug were different from those patients that did not receive the drug.

STATISTICS FOR COLLEGE STUDENTS AND RESEARCHERS

The p value of AxB, the interaction
is p>.05, We read this as follows:
p greater than five per cent. This
means that if we were to say that
there was significant interaction
between electroshock and drug,
we would be running the chance
of reporting an effect that is not
reliable, not significant, meaning
that if we or someone else were to
do the same experiment again,
most likely would not find a
difference as we did.

As we said earlier the concept of
interaction is a new one for us,
and we need to understand it our
way, at the gut level, as we are
used to.

We will now consider an experiment in
which the interaction is significant.

Example 2 of a 2x2 factorial experiment

A pharmacology graduate student
working on his thesis wanted to
find whether a new chemical,
DOP-Y, which has been shown to
elevate dopamine levels in the
brain, may be beneficial to
depressive patients. He was also
interested to see if electroshock
has an effect on these patients
when combined with DOP-Y.
He randomly selected 20
depressive patients, and randomly
assigned them to 4 groups:

electroshock - DOP-Y,
electroshock-no DOP-Y
no-electroshock - DOP-Y,
no-electroshock-no DOP-Y

STATISTICS FOR COLLEGE STUDENTS AND RESEARCHERS

The layout of the pharmacology experiment

	DOP-Y	**no DOP-Y**
electroshock	subject 1 subject 2 subject 3 subject 4 subject 5	subject 6 subject 7 subject 8 subject 9 subject 10
no electroshock	subject 11 subject 12 subject 13 subject 14 subject 15	subject 16 subject 17 subject 18 subject 19 subject 20

The data he recorded are given in
the next table.

High numbers indicate improvement.

STATISTICS FOR COLLEGE STUDENTS AND RESEARCHERS

The data of the pharmacology experiment

	DOP-Y	no DOP-Y
electoshock	52 49 55 50 54 mean = 52 variance = 6.5	33 35 30 32 34 mean = 32.8 variance = 3.7
no electroshock	40 39 38 41 39 mean = 39.4 variance = 1.3	10 13 17 11 14 mean = 13 variance = 7.5

STATISTICS FOR COLLEGE STUDENTS AND RESEARCHERS

THE PHARMACOLOGY EXPERIMENT
ANOVA SUMMARY TABLE

Source	SS	df	MS	F	p
Between A	1312.2	1	1312.2	276.25	<.0001
Between B	2599.2	1	2599.2	547.2	<.0001
A x B *	64.8	1	64.8	13.64	<0.005
Within	76	16	4.75		
Total	4052.2	19			

In this table we see that A, B, and AxB are significant.

Significance in A means that electroshock benefited the depressive patients.

Significance in B means that drug benefited the depressive patients.

Significance in AxB means that there was an interaction between electroshock and drug.

Not clear, you say,

You are correct.

Let us look at the graph of the interaction.
First, we observe that the two lines, shock and no shock, are not parallel. Every time we have an interaction, the two lines are not parallel.

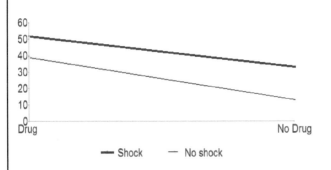

Every time we have an interaction, the two lines are not parallel.

*How about getting to understand
interaction at the gut level, not just
with words?* you say.

Let's do it. Look at the graph
above (previous page).

First, we will visualize the graph
without the effects of the drug. In
that graph the two lines would be
parallel.

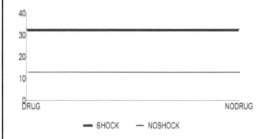

Now visualize the effect of drug as
a force pushing the lines up.
Logically we would expect to see

both lines pushed up while
maintaining the distance between
them, i.e., the two lines may move
higher on the graph, but they
should remain parallel. However,
in the present experiment we saw
that the drug has pushed the no
electroshock line
disproportionately higher.
This is the concept of interaction.

Looking farther out in the ANOVA ocean

There is no limit in the number and complexity of experimental designs. ANOVA lends itself to analysis of these experiments, provided certain constraints are observed during the planning of the experiment.

The concepts in these designs are the same concepts that we developed in this book.

Complex designs are used more often in psychological and social science, and less often in biological, medical sciences. Quite frequently a t-test is used, often illegitimately. We should remember what we said in the beginning of this book. Statistics is a game for the statistician. We use it only if we need it, and should not allow our research to be subjugated to statistics. This is

a vastly important issue. However, it
does not belong to a book like the
present one, whose only ambition
is to demystify statistics and allow
everyone to understand it.

Lecture 8

Repeated measures,

correlated groups

We have already developed the
concept of independence. In those
experiments in which each subject
is used only in one group or
condition, we say that the groups
are independent. So far in this
book we have considered only
independent-groups statistical
designs and experiments.

In designs in which the groups are
not independent, a subject is used

in more than one group or treatment.
That is, each subject experiences
more than one treatment.

For example, John may first be
given behavioral therapy, and
later, several months later, he may
also be given psychoanalytic
therapy. The effects of the two
therapies are then compared.

A variation of this arrangement is
to match each subject with
another subject on the basis of
similarity in some measure. This is
done to eliminate carryover effects
that may, obviously, be present in
giving one subject both treatments.

There are obviously advantages
and disadvantages in choosing
matched groups designs over
independent groups designs.
However, this issue is beyond the
goals of the present book. In
general, independent groups

designs are safer, and should, in
my opinion, be preferred.

The concepts in matched groups
designs are the same as those in
independent groups designs. We
will, therefore, confine ourselves to
giving examples of these designs.
First an example for t-test, and
then an example for ANOVA
repeated measures.

An example of t-test for matched groups

In comparing two new anti-anxiety
drugs, a pharmaceutical company
selected 5 pairs of patients, each
pair matched on the basis of their
anxiety score.

Here is the layout and data of the
experiment.

STATISTICS FOR COLLEGE STUDENTS AND RESEARCHERS

Subject	Difference Score
Tom and Susan	-1
Mike and Jim	-2
Anna and Mary	2
Jerry and Nick	1
George and Kim	-2

Mean for difference=0.4

The formula for the t-test for dependent groups is

$$t_{paired} = \frac{\bar{X}_D}{\sqrt{\dfrac{s^2}{n}}}$$

We read it as follows:

t for paired observations equals
mean of differences divided by the
standard deviation over the square
root of the n. (The standard
deviation divided by the square
root of the n is the standard error
of the mean, SEM, remember?)

You know all of the terms of the
t-formula. You also recognize that it
is the same old story, our old
friend, the z formula.

$t = +0.49$ df=4

Entering the t-table with df 10 we
find that the required t=2.132

Our obtained t 0.49 is smaller
than the required, therefore we do
not have significance. We say that
the difference we observed is not

significant (p>0.05).

STATISTICS FOR COLLEGE STUDENTS AND RESEARCHERS

Study the table below..
It adds to our effort toward integration and understanding beyond a mechanistic use of a plethora of formulas.

Review

I juxtapose the three relevant formulas here for you to compare:

$$t_{paired} = \frac{\bar{X}_D}{\sqrt{\frac{s^2}{n}}}$$

$$SEM = \frac{\sigma}{\sqrt{n}}$$

$$t_{paired} = \frac{\bar{X}_D}{\sqrt{\frac{s^2}{n}}}$$

STATISTICS FOR COLLEGE STUDENTS
AND RESEARCHERS

STATISTICS FOR COLLEGE STUDENTS AND RESEARCHERS

Example of ANOVA Repeated Measures

Four patients with damage in the hippocampus were treated with two new drugs in order to see if their memory improved.

Here is the layout as well as the scores of the experiment. High scores indicate improvement in memory.

Subject	Drug 1	Drug 2
Jim	5	8
Leo	3	9
Alice	6	7
Michel	4	6

ANOVA SUMMARY TABLE
Repeated Measures

Source	SS	df	MS	F	p
Between Columns	18	1	18	7.71	>0.05
Between Rows	3	3			
Error	7	3	2.33		
Total	28	7			

Entering the F table in Appendix with df 1 and 3, we find an F of 10.12. This is the required F in order to have significance. Our obtained F (see ANOVA summary table above) is 7.71. It is less than the required F, therefore, we do not have significance. We say:

There was no significant difference

between the means of the two
conditions (p>0.05).
P greater than point o five.

I see there are questions.
What is Between Columns? You ask.
It is the usual Between variance
that you know. The variance that
our treatments produce. The
variance of the means.

What is Between Rows? you ask.

If you look at the layout above,
you see that the rows are subjects,
one subject per row. The mean of
each subject is the mean of each
row. The variance of these means
are the variance between the
rows.

*Why you did not calculate an F for
the Rows?* you ask.

There is no reason that I can think
of, that would justify my wanting to
know whether there is a statistical

significant difference between subjects. That would be an absurd statement.

Once again you see that our conceptual approach allowed us to attack this design too, without the need for new formulas. What is of course more important is the fact that we understand the logic of this design too. We feel in command, comfortable to handle any issue.

Lecture 9

Complex, mixed, split-plot designs

Elegant research avoids complex
designs also called *split-plot* designs
or mixed designs. However, you may not
be spared of these monsters in your
student or research life.

Let's get a whiff of these monsters.
A psychiatrist wanted to see, if two
new drugs improve the condition
of depressive and schizophrenic
patients.

He randomly assigned 4
depressive patients to Drug1 and

Drug2 conditions. That is, each of the depressive patients will be serving as a subject in both the Drug conditions. This is a repeated measures design.
He did the same with the schizophrenic patients. He randomly assign 4 schizophrenic patients to Drug1 and Drug2 conditions. That is, each of the schizophrenic patients will be serving as a subject in both the Drug conditions. This is a repeated measures design.

As you see, here we have two independent groups (depressive patients, and schizophrenic patients) but each patient is given two treatments, that is he is tested repeatedly, i.e., in both drug conditions. We have a hybrid situation, you would say. Both independence and non-independence in the same experiment.

STATISTICS FOR COLLEGE STUDENTS AND RESEARCHERS

Here is the layout; X stands for scores.

	Drug1	Drug2
Depressive Patients		
Subject 1	X	X
Subject 2	X	X
Subject 3	X	X
Subject 4	X	X
Schizophrenic Patients		
Subject 5	X	X
Subject 6	X	X
Subject 7	X	X
Subject 8	x	x

The analysis of data in complex designs like the above, is, as always, an operation involving the calculation of variance. The interpretation of the results of such an analysis is like the interpretations we considered in this book so far.

ANOVA mixed split plot - formula and practice example

What is ANOVA mixed split plot design

ANOVA mixed split plot designs are complex designs that employ both independent and repeated measures. The best way to explain this is to present the layout of these experimental designs.

STATISTICS FOR COLLEGE STUDENTS AND RESEARCHERS

TABLE SHOWING THE LAYOUT

OF MIXED SPLIT-PLOT DESIGNS

Subjects	Drug 1	Drug 2
DEPRESSIVE		
1	50	68
2	55	63
3	56	65
4	50	67
5	56	69
6	54	68
SCHIZOPHRENIC		
7	99	122
8	100	125
9	110	130
10	90	135
11	105	140
12	115	131

Observe that there are two independent groups, depressive, and schizophrenic. Also observe that each subject of the depressive and schizophrenic groups is repeatedly tested, once with Drug 1, and later with Drug 2. This is a repeated measures arrangement So here we have a design in which independent and repeated measures are mixed. The name split plot comes from the fact that this design is extensively used in agricultural research.

ANOVA mixed split plot designs formula

As in all ANOVA, the formula for these designs is:

$$F = \frac{MS_{between}}{MS_{within}}$$

We read this as follows: Mean square between over mean square within. What is mean square, you ask? It is the mean of squares. What is squares, you ask. Squares is the statistical term for squared deviations (of squared differences) of each score X from the mean. What are the squared differences, you ask. Remember the formula for variance?

$$s^2 = \frac{\sum (X - \bar{X})^2}{n - 1}$$

Look at the numerator

$$\sum (X - \bar{X})^2$$

These are the squared differences summed. To complete our reasoning, we go back to where we started, the F formula, or F ratio, the formula for ANOVA. Why mean sums of squares? Simple because like all averages, we divide by the number of scores. If you are observant, you will notice that the F formula is a modified t formula.

FORMAT OF ANOVA MIXED SPIT PLOT SUMMARY TABLE

SOURCE	SS	df	MS	F	p
Between Independent					
B	*	*	*	*	*
Error	*	*	*		
Total	*	*			
Between repeated measures					
A	*	*	*	*	*
AxB	*	*	*		*
Error	*	*	*		
Total		*			
TOTAL		*			

STATISTICS FOR COLLEGE STUDENTS AND RESEARCHERS

HOW TO CALCULATE df OF ANOVA MIXED SPIT PLOT SUMMARY TABLE

SOURCE	SS	df	MS	F	p
Between Independent					
B		number of independent groups minus 1	*	*	*
Error		total number of subjects minus the number of independent groups	*		
Total		total number of subjects minus 1			
Between repeated measures					
A	*	number of repetitions minus 1	*	*	*
AxB	*	df A x df B	*		*
Error	*	error between independent x number of repetitions	*		
Total		*			
TOTAL		total number of scores minus 1			

STATISTICS FOR COLLEGE STUDENTS
AND RESEARCHERS

ANOVA mixed split plot- practice examples

ANOVA mixed split plot- practice example 1

An experimenter wanted to test drugs (factor A), Drug 1 (A1) and Drug 2 (A2) for their effect on serotonin level in the blood of patients (factor B) suffering from depression (B1) and schizophrenia (B2) . He randomly selected six patients suffering from depression and gave them Drug 1. He waited for one hour and then he measured the level of serotonin in nanograms per liter (ng/lt) of each subject. He recorded the data. One week later he gave these subjects Drug 2. He waited for one hour and measured the level of serotonin of each subject. He also randomly selected six patients suffering from schizophrenia and repeated the same experiment that he performed with the depressive patients. The data are presented in the table below.

STATISTICS FOR COLLEGE STUDENTS AND RESEARCHERS

STATISTICS FOR COLLEGE STUDENTS AND RESEARCHERS

	Subjects	A1 Drug 1	A2 Drug 2
	DEPRESSIVE		
	1	50	68
	2	55	63
B1	3	56	65
	4	50	67
	5	56	69
	6	54	68
	SCHIZOPHRENIC		
	7	99	122
	8	100	125
B2	9	110	130
	10	90	135
	11	105	140
	12	115	131

STATISTICS FOR COLLEGE STUDENTS AND RESEARCHERS

ANOVA MIXED SPIT PLOT SUMMARY TABLE

SOURCE	SS	df	MS	F	p
Between Independent					
B		1			
Error		10			
Total		11			
Between repeated measures					
A		1			
AxB		1			
Error		10			
Total		12			
TOTAL		23			

STATISTICS FOR COLLEGE STUDENTS AND RESEARCHERS

ANOVA mixed split plot- practice example 2

An experimenter wanted to test two new drugs for their effect on body temperature in three age groups: Young (20-30), Middle age (40-50), Old (70-80. He randomly selected 5 patients from each of these age groups. He gave Drug 1 to each of the three groups. He waited for one hour and then he measured the body temperature of each subject using a Celsius thermometer. He recorded the data. One week later he gave these subjects Drug 2. He waited for one hour and measured the temperature of each subject.. The data are presented in the table below.

STATISTICS FOR COLLEGE STUDENTS AND RESEARCHERS

	Subjects	A1 Drug 1	A2 Drug 2
B1	YOUNG 1 2 3 4 5	37.0 37.1 37.3 37.4 37.4	37.6 37.5 37.4 37.4 37.6
B2	MIDDLE AGE 6 7 8 9 10	37.1 37.2 37.4 37,6 375	37.8 37.7 37.6 37.8 37.8
B3	OLD 11 12 13 14 15	37.7 37.8 37.8 37.8 37.9	38.1 38.3 37.9 38.0 38.5

STATISTICS FOR COLLEGE STUDENTS AND RESEARCHERS

STATISTICS FOR COLLEGE STUDENTS AND RESEARCHERS

The summary table of the ANOVA follows.

ANOVA SUMMARY TABLE

SOURCE	SS	df	MS	F	p
Between Independent					
B		2			
Error		12			
Total		14			
Between repeated measures					
A		1			
AxB		2			
Error		12			
Total		15			
TOTAL		29			

PART 3. STATISTICAL DESIGN

Identify the design-case 1

A psychologist wanted to find the kind of movie, crime movie or extreme adventure, that produces greater anxiety in college students. He used two groups of subjects: one viewed a crime movie, and the other viewed an adventure movie. He recorded the Galvanic skin response (GSR) during the movies and took the maximal response (millivolts) as data. Identify the statistical design. Give your answer in the comments space below.

Identify the design-case 2

A psychologist wanted to find the kind of movie, crime movie or extreme adventure, produces anxiety in college students. He used two groups of subjects: one viewed a crime movie, and the other viewed an adventure movie. He recorded the facial expression of the students during the movie and rated it as anxious or non-anxious. Identify the statistical design. Give your answer in the comments space below.

Identify the design-case 3

A psychiatrist wanted to test the effects of
two new drugs on serotonin levels of
schizophrenic patients. He randomly
selected 20 schizophrenic patients and
randomly assigned them to two groups, 10
patients per group. Group 1 received Drug 1,
Group 2 received Drug 2. Ten hours later he
measured the content of serotonin in the
patients blood in nano liters. Identify the
statistical design. Give your answer in the
comments space below.

Identify the design-case 4

A psychiatrist wanted to test the effects of three new drugs on serotonin levels of schizophrenic patients. He randomly selected 30 schizophrenic patients and randomly assigned them to three groups 10 patients per group. Group 1 received Drug 1, Group 2 received Drug 2, Group 3 received Drug 3. Ten hours later he measured the content of serotonin in the patients blood in nano liters. Identify the statistical design. Give your answer in the comments space below.

Identify the design-case 5

A psychiatrist wanted to test the effects of a new drug on serotonin levels of schizophrenic and depressive patients. He randomly selected 10 schizophrenic patients and 10 depressive patients and gave them the drug. Ten hours later he measured the content of serotonin in the patients blood in nano liters. Identify the statistical design. Give your answer in the comments space below.

Identify the design-case 6

A psychiatrist wanted to test the effects of four new drugs on serotonin levels of schizophrenic patients. He randomly selected 40 schizophrenic patients and randomly assigned them to four groups 10 patients per group. Group 1 received Drug 1, Group 2 received Drug 2, Group 3 received Drug 3, Group 4 received Drug 4. Ten hours later he measured the content of serotonin in the patients blood in nano liters. Identify the statistical design. Give your answer in the comments space below.

Identify the design-case 7

A psychiatrist wanted to test the effects of two new drugs on serotonin levels of schizophrenic patients. He randomly selected 30 schizophrenic patients and gave them Drug 1. Ten hours later he measured the content of serotonin in the patients blood in nano liters.A month later, he gave the same patients Drug 2. Ten hours later he measured the content of serotonin in the patients blood in nano liters. Identify the statistical design. Give your answer in the comments space below.

Identify the design-case 8

A psychiatrist wanted to test the effects of two new drugs on serotonin levels of schizophrenic and depressive patients. He randomly selected 10 schizophrenic patients and 10 depressive patients and gave them Drug 1. Ten hours later he measured the content of serotonin in the patients blood in nano liters. A month later he gave these patients Drug 2. Ten hours later he measured the content of serotonin in the patients blood in nano liters. Identify the statistical design. Give your answer in the comments space below.

Identify the design-case 9

A psychiatrist wanted to test the effects of a new drug on echolalia (echolalia is the behavior of repeating what you hear, as in echo) of schizophrenic patients. He randomly selected 30 schizophrenic patients and randomly assigned them to two groups 15 patients per group. Group 1 received a no-drug substance (placebo), Group 2 received the Drug. Ten hours later he tested the patients and counted the patients who showed echolalia. Identify the statistical design. Give your answer in the comments space below.

Identify the design-case 10

A psychiatrist wanted to test the effects of two new drugs on serotonin levels of schizophrenic and depressive patients. He randomly selected 20 schizophrenic patients and randomly assigned them to two groups, Group 1 and Group 2, 10 patients per group. He also randomly selected 20 depressive patients and randomly assigned them to two groups, Group 3 and Group 4, 10 patients per group. He then gave Drug 1 to Group 1 and Group 3, he also gave Drug 2 to Group 2 and Group 4. Ten hours later he measured the content of serotonin in the patient's blood in nano liters. Identify the statistical design. Give your answer in the comments space below.

Identify the design-case 11

A psychiatrist wanted to test the effects of three new drugs on echolalia (echolalia is the behavior of repeating what you hear, as in echo) of schizophrenic patients. He randomly selected 30 schizophrenic patients and randomly assigned them to three groups, 10 patients per group. Group 1 received Drug 1, Group 2 received Drug 2, Group 3 received Drug 3. Ten hours later he tested the patients and counted the patients who showed echolalia. Identify the statistical design. Give your answer in the comments space below.

Identify the design-case 12

Study the experiment described below and
answer these questions:
1. Identify the design.
2 Which statistical test will the experimenter
run?
3. When the experimenter will publish his
findings, will he report a p value?

A pharmacologist wanted to test the effects
of a new drug on general behavioral arousal.
He used three hamsters. The measure of
arousal was spontaneous running activity in
a running wheel. In phase A, he recorded
daily wheel turns for 10 days. In phase B, he
gave the hamsters the drug daily and
recorded their wheel running for 10 days. In
the third phase he reintroduced phase A, that
is he withdrew the drug and recorded the
running activity of the hamsters for 10 days.

Identify the design-case 13

A psychiatrist wanted to test the effects of four new drugs on schizophrenic patients. He randomly selected 40 schizophrenic patients and randomly assigned them to four groups 10 patients per group. Group 1 received Drug 1, Group 2 received Drug 2, Group 3 received Drug 3, Group 4 received Drug 4. At the end of a thirty day treatment with these drugs, he gave the patients a test that measured incidence of psychotic behavior. He reported his findings in graphs showing the number of patients in each group that showed improvement. Identify the statistical design. Give your answer in the comments space below.

STATISTICS FOR COLLEGE STUDENTS AND RESEARCHERS

PART 4. PRACTICE
EXERCISES

The mean: practice exercises and

solutions

The problem: A high school teacher gave a history exam to her class of ten students. She graded the papers and recorded the score of each student. She then decided to calculate the mean of these scores.

X 19 20 18 13 16 17 20 28 16 18

To calculate the mean we add up all the scores and divide by the number of scores. Here is the formula for the mean.

$$\bar{X} = \frac{\sum X}{n}$$

The solution

Variance: practice exercises and

solution

Variance is a measure of variability, the
degree to which scores (X) vary. More
precisely, variance measures the degree
scores deviate from the mean.

The problem

A college coach recorded in seconds the
time it took ten freshmen to run 100 meters.
He wanted to know the degree scores vary.
He calculated the mean of these scores. Next
he calculated the variance, that is how far
from the mean the scores were located.

X
17
20
18
15
18
17
15
14
16
19

STATISTICS FOR COLLEGE STUDENTS AND RESEARCHERS

To calculate the mean we add up all the scores and divide by the number of scores. Here is the formula for the mean.

$$\bar{X} = \frac{\sum X}{n}$$

$$mean = \frac{sum\,of\,scores}{number\,of\,scores}$$

Next he subtracted each score from the mean, to have the degree of deviation of each score from the mean.

$$X - \bar{X}$$

Next he squared these deviations

$$(X - \bar{X})^2$$

STATISTICS FOR COLLEGE STUDENTS AND RESEARCHERS

Next, he added up these squared deviations. This is the sum of squared deviations, or SS.

$$\sum (X - \bar{X})^2$$

Finally he divided the sum of squares by the number of scores minus 1. This is variance, The formula for variance is:

$$s^2 = \frac{\sum (X - \bar{X})^2}{n - 1}$$

$$variance = \frac{sum of squared deviations}{the number os scores minus 1}$$

The solution

Please calculate the variance and post it as a comment below.

The sum of squares: practice

exercises and solutions

The sum of squares or SS is a term on the ANOVA summary table. It is the sum of squared deviation of scores from the mean.
The problem
A high school teacher gave a history exam to her class of ten students. She graded the papers and recorded the score of each student. She then calculated the mean of these scores. Later she wanted to see how far from the mean the scores were located..

X 19 20 18 13 16 17 20 28 16 18

To calculate the mean we add up all the scores and divide by the number of scores. Here is the formula for the mean.

STATISTICS FOR COLLEGE STUDENTS AND RESEARCHERS

$$\bar{X} = \frac{\sum X}{n}$$

$$mean = \frac{sum\,of\,scores}{number\,of\,scores}$$

Next she subtracted each score from the mean, to have the degree of deviation of each score from the mean.

$$X - \bar{X}$$

Next she squared these deviations

$$(X - \bar{X})^2$$

Finally, she added up these squared

deviations. This is the sum of squared
deviations, or SS.

$$\sum (X - \bar{X})^2$$

The solution

Standard deviation practice

exercises and solutions

Standard deviation is a measure of variability. It is the square root of variance. Variance is a measure of variability, the degree to which scores vary. More precisely, variance measures the degree scores deviate from the mean.

The problem
A college coach recorded in seconds the time it took ten freshmen to run 100 meters. He wanted to know the degree scores vary. He calculated the mean of these scores. Next he calculated the variance, that is how far from the mean the scores were located..Finlay, he calculated the standard deviation

STATISTICS FOR COLLEGE STUDENTS AND RESEARCHERS

X
19
13
17
18
18
19
15
18
14
20

To calculate the mean we add up all the scores and divide by the number of scores. Here is the formula for the mean.

$$\bar{X} = \frac{\sum X}{n}$$

$$mean = \frac{sum\,of\,scores}{number\,of\,scores}$$

Next he subtracted each score from the

mean, to have the degree of deviation of each score from the mean.

$$X - \bar{X}$$

Next he squared these deviations

$$(X - \bar{X})^2$$

Next, he added up these squared deviations. This is the sum of squared deviations, or SS.

$$\sum (X - \bar{X})^2$$

Next, he divided the sum of squares by the number of scores minus 1. This is variance, The formula for variance is:

$$s^2 = \frac{\sum (X - \bar{X})^2}{n - 1}$$

STATISTICS FOR COLLEGE STUDENTS
AND RESEARCHERS

$$variance = \frac{sum of squared deviations}{the numbers scores minus 1}$$

Finally he calculated the standard deviation.

$$s = \sqrt{\frac{\sum (X - \bar{X})^2}{n - 1}}$$

standard deviation =
$$\frac{square root of sum of squares}{number of scores minus 1}$$

The solution

ANOVA mixed split plot- practice example

An experimenter wanted to test two new drugs for their effect on body temperature in three age groups: Young (20-30), Middle age (40-50), Old (70-80. He randomly selected 5 patients from each of these age groups. He gave Drug 1 to each of the three groups. He waited for one hour and then he measured the body temperature of each subject using a Celsius thermometer. He recorded the data. One week later he gave these subjects Drug 2. He waited for one hour and measured the temperature of each subject.. The data are presented in the table below.

STATISTICS FOR COLLEGE STUDENTS AND RESEARCHERS

	Subjects	A1 Drug 1	A2 Drug 2
B1	YOUNG		
	1	37.0	37.6
	2	37.1	37.5
	3	37.3	37.4
	4	37.4	37.4
	5	37.4	37.6
B2	MIDDLE AGE		
	6	37.1	37.8
	7	37.2	37.7
	8	37.4	37.6
	9	37,6	37.8
	10	375	37.8
B3	OLD		
	11	37.7	38.1
	12	37.8	38.3
	13	37.8	37.9
	14	37.8	38.0
	15	37.9	38.5

STATISTICAL DESIGN QUESTIONS

Statistical design practice question 1

Study the following table and answer these questions:

1 What is the design?
2. How many independent groups are there in this experiment?
3. How many repeated measures for each subject are there in this experiment?
4. What is the total number of subjects in this experiment?
5. How many subjects were there in each group?

6. Was the finding of this experiment
statistically *significant?*
7. What does p<0.0001 mean?
8. Is there a mistake in this table?

Source	SS	df	MS	F	p
Between	1259	2	629.6	20.24	<0.0001
Within	373.2	12	31.10		
Total	1632	14			

Statistical design practice

question 2

Study the following table and answer these
questions:

1 What is the design?
2. How many independent groups are there
in this experiment?
3. How many repeated measures for each
subject are there in this experiment?
4. What is the total number of subjects in
this experiment?
5. How many subjects were there in each
group?
6. Was the finding of this experiment
statistically *significant?*
7. What does p<0.0001 mean?
8. Is there a mistake in this table?

STATISTICS FOR COLLEGE STUDENTS AND RESEARCHERS

Source	SS	df	MS	F	p
Between	1259	2	629.6	100.24	<0.0001
Within	373.2	12	31.10		
Total	1632	14			

APPENDIX

STATISTICS FOR COLLEGE STUDENTS
AND RESEARCHERS

STATISTICS FOR COLLEGE STUDENTS
AND RESEARCHERS

Five simple formulas for all

parametric statistics

List of the five simple formulas that you
need for parametric Statistics.

These are the five formulas that you need in
order to analyze your data at college as well
as graduate school and post doc work.

STATISTICS FOR COLLEGE STUDENTS AND RESEARCHERS

Mean formula $\quad \bar{X} = \dfrac{\sum X}{n}$

Variance formula $\quad s^2 = \dfrac{\sum (X - \bar{X})^2}{n - 1}$

t – test formula $\quad t = \dfrac{\bar{X}_1 - \bar{X}_2}{\sqrt{\dfrac{s_1^2}{n_1}} + \sqrt{\dfrac{s_2^2}{n_2}}}$

Paired t – test formula $\quad t_{paired} = \dfrac{\bar{X}_D}{\sqrt{\dfrac{s^2}{n}}}$

F ratio formula $\quad F = \dfrac{MS_{between}}{MS_{within}}$

STATISTICS FOR COLLEGE STUDENTS
AND RESEARCHERS

Statistical

Tables

STATISTICS FOR COLLEGE STUDENTS
AND RESEARCHERS

The Normal Distribution Table
How to use this table,

The first left column begins with 00
and ends with **3.0** This column
refers to standard deviation, or z.

The first, top line

0.00 0.01 0.02 0.03 0.04 0.05 0.06 0.07 0.08 0.09

simply adds decimals to the
column. E.g., 1 on the left column
increased to 1.01 1.02 all the
way to 109 and then you shift to
the next line, 1.1

Example: Place your finger at 1.9
on the first left column. Draw your
finger horizontally to the seventh
column. You read 0.4750 . This
means that between the mean and
standard deviation or z 1.96
47.5% of the area of the curve
lies.

STATISTICS FOR COLLEGE STUDENTS AND RESEARCHERS

The Normal Curve Table

Z	0.00	0.01	0.02	0.03	0.04	0.05	0.06	0.07	0.08	0.09
0.0	0.0000	0.0040	0.0080	0.0120	0.0160	0.0199	0.0239	0.0279	0.0319	0.0359
0.1	0.0398	0.0438	0.0478	0.0517	0.0557	0.0596	0.0636	0.0675	0.0714	0.0753
0.2	0.0793	0.0832	0.0871	0.0910	0.0948	0.0987	0.1026	0.1064	0.1103	0.1141
0.3	0.1179	0.1217	0.1255	0.1293	0.1331	0.1368	0.1406	0.1443	0.1480	0.1517
0.4	0.1554	0.1591	0.1628	0.1664	0.1700	0.1736	0.1772	0.1808	0.1844	0.1879
0.5	0.1915	0.1950	0.1985	0.2019	0.2054	0.2088	0.2123	0.2157	0.2190	0.2224
0.6	0.2257	0.2291	0.2324	0.2357	0.2389	0.2422	0.2454	0.2486	0.2517	0.2549
0.7	0.2580	0.2611	0.2642	0.2673	0.2704	0.2734	0.2764	0.2794	0.2823	0.2852
0.8	0.2881	0.2910	0.2939	0.2967	0.2995	0.3023	0.3051	0.3078	0.3106	0.3133
0.9	0.3159	0.3186	0.3212	0.3238	0.3264	0.3289	0.3315	0.3340	0.3365	0.3389
1.0	0.3413	0.3438	0.3461	0.3485	0.3508	0.3531	0.3554	0.3577	0.3599	0.3621
1.1	0.3643	0.3665	0.3686	0.3708	0.3729	0.3749	0.3770	0.3790	0.3810	0.3830
1.2	0.3849	0.3869	0.3888	0.3907	0.3925	0.3944	0.3962	0.3980	0.3997	0.4015
1.3	0.4032	0.4049	0.4066	0.4082	0.4099	0.4115	0.4131	0.4147	0.4162	0.4177
1.4	0.4192	0.4207	0.4222	0.4236	0.4251	0.4265	0.4279	0.4292	0.4306	0.4319
1.5	0.4332	0.4345	0.4357	0.4370	0.4382	0.4394	0.4406	0.4418	0.4429	0.4441
1.6	0.4452	0.4463	0.4474	0.4484	0.4495	0.4505	0.4515	0.4525	0.4535	0.4545
1.7	0.4554	0.4564	0.4573	0.4582	0.4591	0.4599	0.4608	0.4616	0.4625	0.4633
1.8	0.4641	0.4649	0.4656	0.4664	0.4671	0.4678	0.4686	0.4693	0.4699	0.4706
1.9	0.4713	0.4719	0.4726	0.4732	0.4738	0.4744	0.4750	0.4756	0.4761	0.4767
2.0	0.4772	0.4778	0.4783	0.4788	0.4793	0.4798	0.4803	0.4808	0.4812	0.4817
2.1	0.4821	0.4826	0.4830	0.4834	0.4838	0.4842	0.4846	0.4850	0.4854	0.4857
2.2	0.4861	0.4864	0.4868	0.4871	0.4875	0.4878	0.4881	0.4884	0.4887	0.4890
2.3	0.4893	0.4896	0.4898	0.4901	0.4904	0.4906	0.4909	0.4911	0.4913	0.4916
2.4	0.4918	0.4920	0.4922	0.4925	0.4927	0.4929	0.4931	0.4932	0.4934	0.4936
2.5	0.4938	0.4940	0.4941	0.4943	0.4945	0.4946	0.4948	0.4949	0.4951	0.4952
2.6	0.4953	0.4955	0.4956	0.4957	0.4959	0.4960	0.4961	0.4962	0.4963	0.4964
2.7	0.4965	0.4966	0.4967	0.4968	0.4969	0.4970	0.4971	0.4972	0.4973	0.4974
2.8	0.4974	0.4975	0.4976	0.4977	0.4977	0.4978	0.4979	0.4979	0.4980	0.4981
9	0.4981	0.4982	0.4982	0.4983	0.4984	0.4984	0.4985	0.4985	0.4986	0.4986
3.0	0.4987	0.4987	0.4987	0.4988	0.4988	0.4989	0.4989	0.4989	0.4990	0.4990

STATISTICS FOR COLLEGE STUDENTS AND RESEARCHERS

The t-distribution Table
How to use this table.

The first column on the left of the table refers to degrees of freedom, df.

To find df simply subtract 2 from the number of scores you have in your experiment.

The first, top horizontal line refers to percentage of the t-distribution, the p or level of significance you wish to employ. The 5% level is adequate.

Example: If you have an experiment with 2 independent groups, 10 subject each, your df is 20-2=18

Suppose you analyzed your data, and you found a t = 4.51

Now you enter the t-table. Place your finger on the first, left column on 18 (that is your df).
Next draw your finger to the second column

with the heading 0.05. You find t 1.734
Now compare your t value of t = 4.51 to
that of the table, which is 1.734 You see
that your t is larger than the one in the table.
This means that the finding of your
experiment is significant, $p < 0.05$

STATISTICS FOR COLLEGE STUDENTS AND RESEARCHERS

The t-distribution Table

	0.10	0.05	0.025	0.01	0.005	0.001
1.	3.078	6.314	12.70	31.82	63.65	318.3
2.	1.886	2.920	4.303	6.965	9.925	22.32
3.	1.638	2.353	3.182	4.541	5.841	10.21
4.	1.533	2.132	2.776	3.747	4.604	7.173
5.	1.476	2.015	2.571	3.365	4.032	5.893
6.	1.440	1.943	2.447	3.143	3.707	5.208
7.	1.415	1.895	2.365	2.998	3.499	4.782
8.	1.397	1.860	2.306	2.896	3.355	4.499
9.	1.383	1.833	2.262	2.821	3.250	4.296
10.	1.372	1.812	2.228	2.764	3.169	4.143
11.	1.363	1.796	2.201	2.718	3.106	4.024
12.	1.356	1.782	2.179	2.681	3.055	3.929
13.	1.350	1.771	2.160	2.650	3.012	3.852
14.	1.345	1.761	2.145	2.624	2.977	3.787
15.	1.341	1.753	2.131	2.602	2.947	3.733
16.	1.337	1.746	2.120	2.583	2.921	3.686
17.	1.333	1.740	2.110	2.567	2.898	3.646
18.	1.330	1.734	2.101	2.552	2.878	3.610
19.	1.328	1.729	2.093	2.539	2.861	3.579
20.	1.325	1.725	2.086	2.528	2.845	3.552
21.	1.323	1.721	2.080	2.518	2.831	3.527
22.	1.321	1.717	2.074	2.508	2.819	3.505
23.	1.319	1.714	2.069	2.500	2.807	3.485

STATISTICS FOR COLLEGE STUDENTS
AND RESEARCHERS

24. 1.318 1.711 2.064 2.492 2.797 3.467
25. 1.316 1.708 2.060 2.485 2.787 3.450
26. 1.315 1.706 2.056 2.479 2.779 3.435
27. 1.314 1.703 2.052 2.473 2.771 3.421
28. 1.313 1.701 2.048 2.467 2.763 3.408
29. 1.311 1.699 2.045 2.462 2.756 3.396
30. 1.310 1.697 2.042 2.457 2.750 3.385
31. 1.309 1.696 2.040 2.453 2.744 3.375
32. 1.309 1.694 2.037 2.449 2.738 3.365
33. 1.308 1.692 2.035 2.445 2.733 3.356
34. 1.307 1.691 2.032 2.441 2.728 3.348
35. 1.306 1.690 2.030 2.438 2.724 3.340
36. 1.306 1.688 2.028 2.434 2.719 3.333
37. 1.305 1.687 2.026 2.431 2.715 3.326
38. 1.304 1.686 2.024 2.429 2.712 3.319
39. 1.304 1.685 2.023 2.426 2.708 3.313
40. 1.303 1.684 2.021 2.423 2.704 3.307
41. 1.303 1.683 2.020 2.421 2.701 3.301
42. 1.302 1.682 2.018 2.418 2.698 3.296
43. 1.302 1.681 2.017 2.416 2.695 3.291
44. 1.301 1.680 2.015 2.414 2.692 3.286
45. 1.301 1.679 2.014 2.412 2.690 3.281
46. 1.300 1.679 2.013 2.410 2.687 3.277
47. 1.300 1.678 2.012 2.408 2.685 3.273
48. 1.299 1.677 2.011 2.407 2.682 3.269
49. 1.299 1.677 2.010 2.405 2.680 3.265
50. 1.299 1.676 2.009 2.403 2.678 3.261

STATISTICS FOR COLLEGE STUDENTS AND RESEARCHERS

51. 1.298 1.675 2.008 2.402 2.676 3.258
52. 1.298 1.675 2.007 2.400 2.674 3.255
53. 1.298 1.674 2.006 2.399 2.672 3.251
54. 1.297 1.674 2.005 2.397 2.670 3.248
55. 1.297 1.673 2.004 2.396 2.668 3.245
56. 1.297 1.673 2.003 2.395 2.667 3.242
57. 1.297 1.672 2.002 2.394 2.665 3.239
58. 1.296 1.672 2.002 2.392 2.663 3.237
59. 1.296 1.671 2.001 2.391 2.662 3.234
60. 1.296 1.671 2.000 2.390 2.660 3.232
61. 1.296 1.670 2.000 2.389 2.659 3.229
62. 1.295 1.670 1.999 2.388 2.657 3.227
63. 1.295 1.669 1.998 2.387 2.656 3.225
64. 1.295 1.669 1.998 2.386 2.655 3.223
65. 1.295 1.669 1.997 2.385 2.654 3.220
66. 1.295 1.668 1.997 2.384 2.652 3.218
67. 1.294 1.668 1.996 2.383 2.651 3.216
68. 1.294 1.668 1.995 2.382 2.650 3.214
69. 1.294 1.667 1.995 2.382 2.649 3.213
70. 1.294 1.667 1.994 2.381 2.648 3.211
71. 1.294 1.667 1.994 2.380 2.647 3.209
72. 1.293 1.666 1.993 2.379 2.646 3.207
73. 1.293 1.666 1.993 2.379 2.645 3.206
74. 1.293 1.666 1.993 2.378 2.644 3.204
75. 1.293 1.665 1.992 2.377 2.643 3.202
76. 1.293 1.665 1.992 2.376 2.642 3.201
77. 1.293 1.665 1.991 2.376 2.641 3.199

STATISTICS FOR COLLEGE STUDENTS AND RESEARCHERS

78. 1.292 1.665 1.991 2.375 2.640 3.198
79. 1.292 1.664 1.990 2.374 2.640 3.197
80. 1.292 1.664 1.990 2.374 2.639 3.195
81. 1.292 1.664 1.990 2.373 2.638 3.194
82. 1.292 1.664 1.989 2.373 2.637 3.193
83. 1.292 1.663 1.989 2.372 2.636 3.191
84. 1.292 1.663 1.989 2.372 2.636 3.190
85. 1.292 1.663 1.988 2.371 2.635 3.189
86. 1.291 1.663 1.988 2.370 2.634 3.188
87. 1.291 1.663 1.988 2.370 2.634 3.187
88. 1.291 1.662 1.987 2.369 2.633 3.185
89. 1.291 1.662 1.987 2.369 2.632 3.184
90. 1.291 1.662 1.987 2.368 2.632 3.183
91. 1.291 1.662 1.986 2.368 2.631 3.182
92. 1.291 1.662 1.986 2.368 2.630 3.181
93. 1.291 1.661 1.986 2.367 2.630 3.180
94. 1.291 1.661 1.986 2.367 2.629 3.179
95. 1.291 1.661 1.985 2.366 2.629 3.178
96. 1.290 1.661 1.985 2.366 2.628 3.177
97. 1.290 1.661 1.985 2.365 2.627 3.176
98. 1.290 1.661 1.984 2.365 2.627 3.175
99. 1.290 1.660 1.984 2.365 2.626 3.175
100. 1.290 1.660 1.984 2.364 2.626 3.174

∞ 1.282 1.645 1.960 2.326 2.576 3.090

STATISTICS FOR COLLEGE STUDENTS
AND RESEARCHERS

The F Distribution Table
How to use this table

The first, left column is the df of the denominator of the F ratio, or the error term.

The first, top line is the degrees of freedom of the numerator of the F ratio. Example:

In an experiment with 3 groups of 10 subjects each, we have df between 2, and df within 27.

Suppose that we analyzed our data using ANOVA and we found an F=12.54

Now we enter the F table. Place your finger on the first left column at 27, then draw your finger to the third column which has the heading 2. You read the value 3.354

Now you compare your F which was F=12.54 to the F of this table which was 3.354 Your F is bigger, so the finding of your experiment is significant, p<0.05

The F distribution Table 5% significance level

	1	2	3	4	5	6	7	8	9	10
1	161.4	199.5	215.7	224.5	230.1	233.9	236.7	238.8	240.5	241.8
2	18.51	19.00	19.16	19.24	19.29	19.33	19.35	19.37	19.38	19.39
3	10.12	9.552	9.277	9.117	9.013	8.941	8.887	8.845	8.812	8.786
4	7.709	6.944	6.591	6.388	6.256	6.163	6.094	6.041	5.999	5.964
5	6.608	5.786	5.409	5.192	5.050	4.950	4.876	4.818	4.772	4.735
6	5.987	5.143	4.757	4.534	4.387	4.284	4.207	4.147	4.099	4.060
7	5.591	4.737	4.347	4.120	3.972	3.866	3.787	3.726	3.677	3.637
8	5.318	4.459	4.066	3.838	3.687	3.581	3.500	3.438	3.388	3.347
9	5.117	4.256	3.863	3.633	3.482	3.374	3.293	3.230	3.179	3.137
10	4.965	4.103	3.708	3.478	3.326	3.217	3.135	3.072	3.020	2.978
11	4.844	3.982	3.587	3.357	3.204	3.095	3.012	2.948	2.896	2.854
12	4.747	3.885	3.490	3.259	3.106	2.996	2.913	2.849	2.796	2.753F
13	4.667	3.806	3.411	3.179	3.025	2.915	2.832	2.767	2.714	2.671
14	4.600	3.739	3.344	3.112	2.958	2.848	2.764	2.699	2.646	2.602
15	4.543	3.682	3.287	3.056	2.901	2.790	2.707	2.641	2.588	2.544
16	4.494	3.634	3.239	3.007	2.852	2.741	2.657	2.591	2.538	2.494
17	4.451	3.592	3.197	2.965	2.810	2.699	2.614	2.548	2.494	2.450
18	4.414	3.555	3.160	2.928	2.773	2.661	2.577	2.510	2.456	2.412
19	4.381	3.522	3.127	2.895	2.740	2.628	2.544	2.477	2.423	2.378
20	4.351	3.493	3.098	2.866	2.711	2.599	2.514	2.447	2.393	2.348
21	4.325	3.467	3.072	2.840	2.685	2.573	2.488	2.420	2.366	2.321
22	4.301	3.443	3.049	2.817	2.661	2.549	2.464	2.397	2.342	2.297
23	4.279	3.422	3.028	2.796	2.640	2.528	2.442	2.375	2.320	2.275
24	4.260	3.403	3.009	2.776	2.621	2.508	2.423	2.355	2.300	2.255
25	4.242	3.385	2.991	2.759	2.603	2.490	2.405	2.337	2.282	2.236
26	4.225	3.369	2.975	2.743	2.587	2.474	2.388	2.321	2.265	2.220
27	4.210	3.354	2.960	2.728	2.572	2.459	2.373	2.305	2.250	2.204
28	4.196	3.340	2.947	2.714	2.558	2.445	2.359	2.291	2.236	2.190
29	4.183	3.328	2.934	2.701	2.545	2.432	2.346	2.278	2.223	2.177
30	4.171	3.316	2.922	2.690	2.534	2.421	2.334	2.266	2.211	2.165
31	4.160	3.305	2.911	2.679	2.523	2.409	2.323	2.255	2.199	2.153
32	4.149	3.295	2.901	2.668	2.512	2.399	2.313	2.244	2.189	2.142
33	4.139	3.285	2.892	2.659	2.503	2.389	2.303	2.235	2.179	2.133
34	4.130	3.276	2.883	2.650	2.494	2.380	2.294	2.225	2.170	2.123
35	4.121	3.267	2.874	2.641	2.485	2.372	2.285	2.217	2.161	2.114
36	4.113	3.259	2.866	2.634	2.477	2.364	2.277	2.209	2.153	2.106

STATISTICS FOR COLLEGE STUDENTS AND RESEARCHERS

37 4.105 3.252 2.859 2.626 2.470 2.356 2.270 2.201 2.145 2.0
38 4.098 3.245 2.852 2.619 2.463 2.349 2.262 2.194 2.138 2.091
39 4.091 3.238 2.845 2.612 2.456 2.342 2.255 2.187 2.131 2.084
40 4.085 3.232 2.839 2.606 2.449 2.336 2.249 2.180 2.124 2.077
41 4.079 3.226 2.833 2.600 2.443 2.330 2.243 2.174 2.118 2.071
42 4.073 3.220 2.827 2.594 2.438 2.324 2.237 2.168 2.112 2.065
43 4.067 3.214 2.822 2.589 2.432 2.318 2.232 2.163 2.106 2.059
44 4.062 3.209 2.816 2.584 2.427 2.313 2.226 2.157 2.101 2.054
45 4.057 3.204 2.812 2.579 2.422 2.308 2.221 2.152 2.096 2.049
46 4.052 3.200 2.807 2.574 2.417 2.304 2.216 2.147 2.091 2.044
47 4.047 3.195 2.802 2.570 2.413 2.299 2.212 2.143 2.086 2.039
48 4.043 3.191 2.798 2.565 2.409 2.295 2.207 2.138 2.082 2.035
49 4.038 3.187 2.794 2.561 2.404 2.290 2.203 2.134 2.077 2.030
50 4.034 3.183 2.790 2.557 2.400 2.286 2.199 2.130 2.073 2.026
51 4.030 3.179 2.786 2.553 2.397 2.283 2.195 2.126 2.069 2.022
52 4.027 3.175 2.783 2.550 2.393 2.279 2.192 2.122 2.066 2.018
53 4.023 3.172 2.779 2.546 2.389 2.275 2.188 2.119 2.062 2.015
54 4.020 3.168 2.776 2.543 2.386 2.272 2.185 2.115 2.059 2.011
55 4.016 3.165 2.773 2.540 2.383 2.269 2.181 2.112 2.055 2.008
56 4.013 3.162 2.769 2.537 2.380 2.266 2.178 2.109 2.052 2.005
57 4.010 3.159 2.766 2.534 2.377 2.263 2.175 2.106 2.049 2.001
58 4.007 3.156 2.764 2.531 2.374 2.260 2.172 2.103 2.046 1.998
59 4.004 3.153 2.761 2.528 2.371 2.257 2.169 2.100 2.043 1.995
60 4.001 3.150 2.758 2.525 2.368 2.254 2.167 2.097 2.040 1.993
61 3.998 3.148 2.755 2.523 2.366 2.251 2.164 2.094 2.037 1.990
62 3.996 3.145 2.753 2.520 2.363 2.249 2.161 2.092 2.035 1.987
63 3.993 3.143 2.751 2.518 2.361 2.246 2.159 2.089 2.032 1.985
64 3.991 3.140 2.748 2.515 2.358 2.244 2.156 2.087 2.030 1.982
65 3.989 3.138 2.746 2.513 2.356 2.242 2.154 2.084 2.027 1.980
66 3.986 3.136 2.744 2.511 2.354 2.239 2.152 2.082 2.025 1.977
67 3.984 3.134 2.742 2.509 2.352 2.237 2.150 2.080 2.023 1.975
68 3.982 3.132 2.740 2.507 2.350 2.235 2.148 2.078 2.021 1.973
69 3.980 3.130 2.737 2.505 2.348 2.233 2.145 2.076 2.019 1.971
70 3.978 3.128 2.736 2.503 2.346 2.231 2.143 2.074 2.017 1.969
71 3.976 3.126 2.734 2.501 2.344 2.229 2.142 2.072 2.015 1.967
72 3.974 3.124 2.732 2.499 2.342 2.227 2.140 2.070 2.013 1.965
73 3.972 3.122 2.730 2.497 2.340 2.226 2.138 2.068 2.011 1.963
74 3.970 3.120 2.728 2.495 2.338 2.224 2.136 2.066 2.009 1.961
75 3.968 3.119 2.727 2.494 2.337 2.222 2.134 2.064 2.007 1.959
76 3.967 3.117 2.725 2.492 2.335 2.220 2.133 2.063 2.006 1.958
77 3.965 3.115 2.723 2.490 2.333 2.219 2.131 2.061 2.004 1.956
78 3.963 3.114 2.722 2.489 2.332 2.217 2.129 2.059 2.002 1.954

STATISTICS FOR COLLEGE STUDENTS
AND RESEARCHERS

79 3.962 3.112 2.720 2.487 2.330 2.216 2.128 2.058 2.001 1.953
80 3.960 3.111 2.719 2.486 2.329 2.214 2.126 2.056 1.999 1.951
81 3.959 3.109 2.717 2.484 2.327 2.213 2.125 2.055 1.998 1.950
82 3.957 3.108 2.716 2.483 2.326 2.211 2.123 2.053 1.996 1.948
83 3.956 3.107 2.715 2.482 2.324 2.210 2.122 2.052 1.995 1.947
84 3.955 3.105 2.713 2.480 2.323 2.209 2.121 2.051 1.993 1.945
85 3.953 3.104 2.712 2.479 2.322 2.207 2.119 2.049 1.992 1.944
86 3.952 3.103 2.711 2.478 2.321 2.206 2.118 2.048 1.991 1.943
87 3.951 3.101 2.709 2.476 2.319 2.205 2.117 2.047 1.989 1.941
88 3.949 3.100 2.708 2.475 2.318 2.203 2.115 2.045 1.988 1.940
89 3.948 3.099 2.707 2.474 2.317 2.202 2.114 2.044 1.987 1.939
90 3.947 3.098 2.706 2.473 2.316 2.201 2.113 2.043 1.986 1.938
91 3.946 3.097 2.705 2.472 2.315 2.200 2.112 2.042 1.984 1.936
92 3.945 3.095 2.704 2.471 2.313 2.199 2.111 2.041 1.983 1.935
93 3.943 3.094 2.703 2.470 2.312 2.198 2.110 2.040 1.982 1.934
94 3.942 3.093 2.701 2.469 2.311 2.197 2.109 2.038 1.981 1.933
95 3.941 3.092 2.700 2.467 2.310 2.196 2.108 2.037 1.980 1.932
96 3.940 3.091 2.699 2.466 2.309 2.195 2.106 2.036 1.979 1.931
97 3.939 3.090 2.698 2.465 2.308 2.194 2.105 2.035 1.978 1.930
98 3.938 3.089 2.697 2.465 2.307 2.193 2.104 2.034 1.977 1.929
99 3.937 3.088 2.696 2.464 2.306 2.192 2.103 2.033 1.976 1.928
100 3.936 3.087 2.696 2.463 2.305 2.191 2.103 2.032 1.975 1.927

STATISTICS FOR COLLEGE STUDENTS
AND RESEARCHERS

Key to the design question

Identify the statistical design-case 1
Single factor, one-way ANOVA.
Things to note:
2 independent groups
Data is interval scale of measurement,
therefore we do not use nonparametric tests
like chi square.
Here we can also run t-test for independent
groups.

Identify the statistical design-case 2
Note that the data is dichotomous,yes or no,
therefore nominal scale of measurement.
Data are frequency scores, how many. We
will use nonparametric tests, chi square.

Identify the design-case 3
Single factor, one-way ANOVA.
Things to note:

2 independent groups
Data is interval scale of measurement,
therefore we do not use nonparametric tests
like chi square.
Here we can also run t-test for independent
groups.

Identify the design-case 4
Single factor, one-way ANOVA.
Things to note:
3 independent groups
Data is interval scale of measurement,
therefore we do not use nonparametric tests
like chi square.
Here we cannot run t-tests.

Identify the design-case 5
Single factor, one-way ANOVA.
Things to note:
2 independent groups
Data is interval scale of measurement,
therefore we do not use nonparametric tests
like chi square.
Here we can also run t-test for independent
groups.

Identify the design-case 6

STATISTICS FOR COLLEGE STUDENTS AND RESEARCHERS

Single factor, one-way ANOVA.
Things to note:
4 independent groups
Data is interval scale of measurement, therefore we do not use nonparametric tests like chi square.
Here we can also run t-test for independent groups.

Identify the design-case 7
Repeated measures ANOVA.
Things to note:
1 independent groups.
Each subject was given two treatments, therefore we have two scores from each subject.
Data is interval scale of measurement, therefore we do not use nonparametric tests like chi square.
Here we can also run t-test for matched groups.

Identify the design-case 8
Mixed design (split plot or complex design) ANOVA

Things to note:
2 independent groups, 2 treatments, each
subject recievng both treatments,therefore
repeatedly tested so no independence here.
So here we have independence and no
independence mixed.
Data is interval scale of measurement,
therefore we do not use nonparametric tests
like chi square.
Here we cannot also run t-test for
independent groups.

Identify the design-case 9
Nonparametric test like contingency tables.
Note that data is frequencies, not interval, so
we cannot run parametric tests like ANOVA
or t-test.

Identify the design-case 10
2x2 factorial design ANOVA
Four independent groups receiving 2
dreatments in factorial fashion.
Data is interval or ratio sscale of
measurement.

Identify the design-case 11
Date is frequencies, not interval. We can

STATISTICS FOR COLLEGE STUDENTS
AND RESEARCHERS

only run nonparametric tests like
contingency tables.

Identify the design-case 12
This not a statistical design. It is a "small-n
design".

Identify the design-case 13
Date is frequencies, not interval. We can
only run nonparametric tests like
contingency tables.

FAQ Frequently Asked Questions

Frequently asked questions by students
and researchers

**1. Q. I have an experiment with 2
independent groups. The scale of
measurement is nominal. Can I
use a t-test?**
A. No, use nonparametric tests

**2. Q. I have an experiment with 2
independent groups. The scale of
measurement is interval. Can I
use a t-test?**
A. Yes

**3. Q. I have an experiment with 2
independent groups. The scale of
measurement is ratio. Can I use
a t-test?**
A. Yes

**4. Q. I have an experiment with 2
independent groups. The scale of
measurement interval. Can I use
ANOVA?**
A. Yes

**5. Q. I have an experiment with 2
independent groups. The scale of
measurement ratio. Can I use
ANOVA?**
A. Yes

**6. Q. I have an experiment with 3
independent groups. The scale of
measurement is interval. Can I
use a t-test?**
A. No. Use ANOVA

**7. Q I have run an experiment with
4 independent groups. 20 male
and 20 female subjects. The
experiment aimed at showing that
drinking red wine may lower
cholesterol. The layout was as
follows:
Male-wine, male-no wine.
Female-wine, female-no wine**

STATISTICS FOR COLLEGE STUDENTS AND RESEARCHERS

There were 10 subjects per group. I think this is a 2x2 factorial, but I do not understand why gender is variable. I did not manipulate it, obviously.

A. Gender is a special class of variable. We call this *subject variable*. While we do not manipulate it ourselves, some other agent has done it, in this case Nature, we analyze these experiments like regular designs. Only in the discussion we should be aware that subject variables are actually packages of variables, and we should be cautious in our conclusions.

8. Q. I have an experiment with 3 independent groups. My data are in the interval scale of measurement. I ran an ANOVA and found significance. Does this mean that (a) mean1 is different from mean 2? (b) mean 1 is different from mean 3? (c) mean 2 is different from mean 3?

A. No. It means that your
treatment has had an effect, but
you do not know where the
difference is. ANOVA does not tell
you that. You need to run one of
the so-called *post hoc tests* or
otherwise called *a posteriori tests,*
in order to pinpoint where the
difference is.

The most frequently used post hoc
tests are: The *Newman-Keuls* test,
Tukey's test, the *Scheffé* test.

**9. Q. I have an experiment with 3
independent groups, ratio scale of
measurement. Can I run post hoc
tests without running ANOVA?**
A. No. First run ANOVA. If you find
significance, then proceed with
post hoc tests.

**10. Q. I have an experiment with
3 independent groups, ratio scale
of measurement. Can I run t-test
repeatedly so that I see which
mean is significantly different from
which mean?**

A.   No. Run a post hoc test.

11. Q. My experiment has three groups. Can I run t-tests to test the difference between mean1 and mean2, mean1 and mean3, mean2 and mean3?
A. No, you can not run repeated t-test. The t-distribution takes into account the application of the test only once. Run a one-way ANOVA.

12. Q: What is the formula for degrees of freedom df?

A. The formula for degrees of freedom (df) is: number of scores that goes into the calculation of the mean minus 1. Important note: In ANOVA we calculate the mean of means. Here df=number of means that goes into the calculation of the mean minus 1.

13. Q: What is the formula for the standard normal curve?

A. The formula that creates the standard normal curve is:

$$y = \frac{1}{\sigma\sqrt{2\pi}} e^{\frac{-(x-\mu)^2}{2\sigma^2}}$$

14. Q: What are z scores?

A. A z score is the standard deviation at which a score lies. The formula for the calculation of the z score is:

$$z = \frac{(X - \bar{X})}{s}$$

Example: A distribution with mean 80 and standard deviation 5, what is the z score for score 90? z=90-80/5=10/5=2

15 Q: What are small-n designs?

A. Small-n designs are non-statistical
experimental designs that employ very few
subjects. They focus on detailed
observations of the behavior of each subject
rather than averages and analysis of subject
variability. They were introduced by
behaviorists of the Skinnerian persuasion

STATISTICS FOR COLLEGE STUDENTS AND RESEARCHERS

.

16 Q: What are post-hoc tests?

A. Post-hoc tests, also called "a posteriori" tests, are statistical tests used for individual comparisons of means after an analysis of variance (ANOVA) has been performed. They are all based on the logic of the need to make it more difficult for attaining statistical significance, since theoretically the more tests one performs the greater the probability of finding significance.

Here is a list of the most frequently used post--hoc tests:

Duncan's new multiple range test (MRT)

Dunn's Multiple Comparison Test.

Fisher's Least Significant Difference (LSD)

Newman-Keuls.test

Scheffé's test

STATISTICS FOR COLLEGE STUDENTS AND RESEARCHERS

The standard normal curve

formula

The equation which generates the
normal distribution:

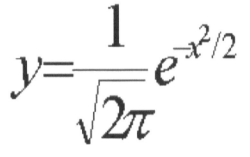

$$y = \frac{1}{\sqrt{2\pi}} e^{-x^2/2}$$

STATISTICS FOR COLLEGE STUDENTS AND RESEARCHERS

STATISTICS FOR COLLEGE STUDENTS AND RESEARCHERS

STORY TITLES

My kids my fingers
No-number numbers
Who's bigger
Working magic with a Goddess
Mathematical sweat
Where does Basita fall?
An archetypal ceremony
Money in a Texas Hat
A Cap for Wisconsin Farmers
Apple-pie IQ
An archetypal ceremony II
Mercy Mr. Gosset
Me minus me equals 1
The long jump
Mean Prophet
Clip his tail
Master of the waves
Beam storm

STATISTICS FOR COLLEGE STUDENTS
AND RESEARCHERS

Epilogue

I hope that you have enjoyed this trip that we took together. I am confident that what you learned here will prove useful in your courses, research, or profession. Above all, it would give me pleasure to know that this book added a tiny little *iota* to your personal philosophy.

STATISTICS FOR COLLEGE STUDENTS AND RESEARCHERS

STATISTICS FOR COLLEGE STUDENTS
AND RESEARCHERS

STATISTICS FOR COLLEGE STUDENTS
AND RESEARCHERS

STATISTICS FOR COLLEGE STUDENTS AND RESEARCHERS

Made in United States
Troutdale, OR
11/08/2024

24581823R00236